EVERYDAY DISCIPLES

EVERYDAY DISCIPLES

Lessons Learned from Unnamed Scripture Heroes

TAYLOR RICKS

SALT LAKE CITY, UTAH

Visit us at deseretbook.com

Library of Congress Cataloging-in-Publication Data

(CIP on file)
ISBN 978-1-63993-006-7

Printed in the United States of America
PubLitho, Draper, UT

10 9 8 7 6 5 4 3 2 1

To my parents and grandparents,
who lived every day seeking to serve and
uplift the one. Their humble examples have taught
me what an "everyday disciple" truly is.

And to my husband, Tanner.
His kindness and example have taught me to
strive to see others more as our Savior does.

CONTENTS

Introduction 1

Come unto Christ 7

Fulfill God's Mission 15

Trust God through the Journey 27

Learn One Another's Stories 40

Pray for Their Enemies 55

Act as Earthly Angels 72

Seek the Light of Christ 94

Remember 105

Give All They Have 121

Carry Others to Christ 132

Fear Not 144

INTRODUCTION

I have always found myself in awe as I've read the scriptures and studied the heroes within their pages. Stories of faith, perseverance, overcoming fear, repentance, and complete reliance on the Savior through unimaginable circumstances have pierced my heart and encouraged me to act.

I began to imagine what it might be like to be one of these heroes in modern day. I wanted to shout my testimony from atop a wall (see Helaman 16:2), encouraging all around to come and hear the message of the restored gospel. I wanted to lead in righteousness and follow the Savior in faith. I wanted to be like the scriptural disciples I revered. I was ready to chop off some arms if it was necessary (see Alma 17:37). I just wanted to be like them.

Ever since I was a little girl, I knew I was a child of God and that He loved me, but I rarely felt like I had a place where I fit in His gospel, or anywhere else. I often felt like I was never quite what I was expected to be. I was too jovial when I should've been more serious, and too serious when others wanted to play. When I was young, I wanted to be surrounded by people who were older than I was, and as I aged, I struggled to find peers with whom I could relate. It was as if I was always in the wrong place at the wrong time and never quite measured up to the expectations I perceived everyone had for me.

I always thought that marriage and motherhood would erase these feelings, but they only intensified them. My husband, children, and I have moved a few times. Each time, we became a part of new wards where all the sisters around me seemed to have made close friendships. Their children would run between houses, they had late-night girls' nights, and they shared inside jokes. They were caring, compassionate, service-oriented, and firm in their testimonies. I was always surrounded by amazing women, and yet week after week, I felt completely alone in my congregations and daily life. At times it seemed as though my efforts and contributions were invisible.

One day, I was sitting in my home office working on a project as tears filled my eyes, and I asked my Heavenly Father why He didn't make room for me in a group of friends in my new ward. I asked Him what was wrong with me. In that moment, the Spirit whispered ever so gently, "If you had made a lot of friends you would be very busy, and you would not be doing the work I need you to do right now." I thought about my family, educational goals, and the volunteer work I was involved in at the time. It all seemed so quiet and behind the scenes. I had never considered that those things were the sacred work that God needed me to do and that my desires could have prevented me from doing that work.

Over the weeks that followed, I began to realize that surely, I wasn't the only person to feel lonely and as though my efforts were trite. Maybe there were others who longed to be a Simon, carrying the cross for the Savior in His final hours (see Mark 15:21), but instead felt like a member of the multitude—loved but seemingly insignificant.

It was then that I realized I was indeed living a life like those in the scripture stories I had come to love, but I had been reading the stories all wrong. Yes, the prophets and those who followed them and preached of truth were truly heroic in their missions, but there were also unnamed disciples in each story. Everywhere I looked, there were people whose faith and diligence pointed to the Savior and whose contributions were pivotal and sacred in the eyes of those they served.

The multitude whom Jesus taught were not simply insignificant bystanders in the story of the Savior's life or a group of people we read quickly past in a verse or two, waiting to learn a greater truth. They were, in fact, quiet, everyday disciples.

Their presence and faithfulness in following the Savior of the world testified of His glory and greatness, simply through coming to hear and heed Him. They stood as a representation of all of us throughout time who would come to hear the message of the Redeemer of the world. They showed everyone in their day that they were willing to sit at the Savior's feet as long as He was willing to speak. They were true followers of the Son of God. They were needed, just as my presence in the Savior's multitude is needed in these latter days—just as your voice in the multitude is needed right alongside mine. In the Savior's ministry and gospel, there are no small parts or insignificant voices.

As Elder Jeffrey R. Holland teaches: "There is room for those who speak different languages, celebrate diverse cultures, and live in a host of locations. There is room for the single, for the married, for large families, and for the childless. There is room for those who once had questions regarding their faith and room for those who still do. There is room for those with differing sexual attractions.

"In short, there is a place for everyone who loves God and honors His commandments as the inviolable measuring rod for personal behavior, for if love of God is the melody of our shared song, surely our common quest to obey Him is the indispensable harmony in it. With divine imperatives of love and faith, repentance and compassion, honesty and forgiveness, there is room in this choir for all who wish to be there" ("Songs Sung and Unsung," *Ensign*, May 2017).

Brothers and sisters, there is room for you, and you are needed here. The Lord needs everyday disciples who defend His name and live the gospel with every ounce of their heart, even if they feel unseen or unknown. He needs women and men who do the right thing when no one is looking and who lift the heavyhearted even if their names remain unwritten. He needs us to know that He has reserved a place for us with Him in His fold, and through our humble acts, we can more fully realize our place there.

As we seek to better exemplify the examples of the quiet, unnamed disciples in the scriptures, we can see that they each faithfully found their place in the fold of God even when their contributions seemed almost completely forgotten or unnoticed by those around them. We may at times feel as though we are forgotten or unnoticed. We might feel called to serve in callings or livelihoods that allow us to fly under the radar, and we might let the adversary whisper to our hearts and minds that God has forgotten us, too. But though it may be small or unseen, the Father's place for you in His heavenly fold is real and tangible. He needs your efforts, just as He needed the efforts of those whose humble, heroic stories are written upon the pages of His holy scriptures.

He has already created a place for you. As you seek and serve Him, obeying His will, you will find you may feel stronger and more secure in that place. It is not required of us to be someone we are not or to traverse paths created for others; we can live in our ordinary places and know that He has a place for us in His fold and kingdom.

The work of the Lord is performed by those who seek

Him in their ordinary circumstances. As President Boyd K. Packer once said: "The Church moves on. It is carried upon the shoulders of worthy members living ordinary lives among ordinary families, guided by the Holy Ghost and the light of Christ, which is in them" ("The Weak and the Simple of the Church," *Ensign*, Nov. 2007).

You may notice that the stories and examples used in this book are familiar; stories heard over many pulpits or like the events you might be experiencing in your own life. I have chosen these with the hope that you can see yourself, your friends, and your families in these stories and learn how your role in this gospel is an important one. But more importantly, as we study and explore these examples together, may we see how all righteous action—regardless of fanfare—preaches, prophesies, and rejoices in Christ (see 2 Nephi 25:26).

Join me on a journey to explore the often unnamed, sometimes forgotten, and seemingly overlooked quiet disciples of the scriptures. Together we will see how they are important members of Christ's multitude and that each testifies of a risen Lord who is "mighty to save" (2 Nephi 31:19).

COME UNTO CHRIST

My sandals sink a little into the dewy earth, but my eyes are fixed forward and upward. Millions of stars dot the sky; I stay focused on one. The brightest one. My heart pounds in anticipation of what we will see below it when we arrive. A tiny, precious King. Just as the prophets had foretold, our Savior is lying in a manger below that bright, bright, star, and I walk alongside fellow believers in our quest to greet Him.

This is how I read scripture.

It is how I have always read it. I like to read it as though I were there, imagining and thinking about the sights, the sounds, the smells, and the pounding in my chest that would testify of the momentous occasion playing out right before me.

I can feel the long grass tickle my arm as the breeze dances through the wave-like blades. The sun kisses my neck, cheeks, and nose while I sit in the field in Cana. Christ's words float across the air and settle in my soul. I know that this is the Son of God.

At the Crucifixion, I feel the darkness and dampness of the sky like a thick, heavy blanket on my skin. The dirt swirling through the air crusts onto my tear-stained cheeks as I kneel at the feet of my Redeemer—of my Jesus. All my duties and cares of the world mean nothing, time stands still, and my heart cries out in utter agony. I wonder if I will ever really be able to take a deep breath again.

It may have felt like that to sit at the base of the cross of the Son of God. But I relate most to what happened in the Americas. It is as though my premortal spirit were there those many years ago and aches to remember every detail as a testimony to my heart of the risen Lord.

Darkness. Three days of complete darkness. I assume it matches the darkness that filled me when the sign of Christ's death came upon us. I yell out in audible distress, my cries echoing through the blackened world and uniting with the cries of my sisters and brothers in the gospel. I missed Him. I looked, I waited, I prayed, I pondered, and still, I missed Him. I can't be consoled; my mind cannot reconcile it. I lie on the filthy ground and cry because I missed meeting Jesus.

Then, almost without warning, comes complete silence to accompany the darkness. Not even the comforting sounds of wind through the trees can be heard for hours (see 3 Nephi 10:2). The blackness completely enfolds me, and though surrounded by so many, it is as if I am completely alone.

The hours pass, and in time, the silence goes with it. The wailing of all who survived echoes again across the land, each cry uniting into one horrifying howl of mourning, until finally the light of day comes (see 3 Nephi 10:8). The only light on the earth. It starts like the head of a pin off in the distant sky, but that is all it takes to overcome the darkness. The light grows steadily, brighter and brighter. I can feel my eyes contract and adjust to the glorious beams flooding over every inch of the once-blackened world. The fourth day has come. The light in the sky miraculously floods into our hearts and finally, we rejoice in our Jesus (see v. 10).

Days pass, but I do not count them; they all seem to become one (see v. 18). Every morning I go to the temple with all who were spared, and we remember our Savior and His sacrifice.

But there is one day I will number in my heart forever. The greatest day. I can hear the small voice off in the distance. It pierces me to my very center, every part of me begins to tremble and shake, and a burning begins in my heart that spreads throughout my body like wildfire (see 3 Nephi 12:3).

Could it be?

A hush falls over us all. The voice comes again, and still, I do not understand. *Oh! How I wish I could understand!* I gather up all the energy of my heart this time. I listen again.

"Behold my Beloved Son, in whom I am well pleased,

in whom I have glorified my name—hear ye Him" (3 Nephi 11:7).

My mind races wildly. *Is it an angel? Did God send us an angel?* But the glorified being speaks, and my eyes blur with tears. I wipe them away, feverishly hoping to see the messenger God has sent.

A voice I know. A voice I remember from before my birth floods my body from the tips of my toes to the top of my head.

"Behold, I am Jesus Christ, whom the prophets testified shall come into the world" (3 Nephi 11:10).

I fall to the earth in humble praise, finally remembering Samuel's prophecies of a risen Lord who would return to us (see v. 12). He is here.

It gives me chills every time. How I wish I could have been there. The multitude went forth and touched His hands, feet, and side and bowed down low before Him in solemn worship. I wonder if I would be able to handle the power that would come from simply touching the hand of Christ—the very hands that healed the leper, turned water into wine, and lifted Lazarus from the dead. The hands that trembled in agony as they atoned for my sins and were pierced and scarred for my transgressions. I wonder if my meager offerings would qualify me to touch such a hand.

I know the answer. I am not qualified at all, but He would welcome me anyway. Though I am imperfect and flawed, Christ would stretch forth His hand to me in perfect love, hoping I would have the faith to reach back, just as He does now.

The days that followed His coming in the Americas had to have been astounding to witness. He gave the authority to baptize, called Apostles, administered the sacrament, established His gospel, taught how to pray in His name, bestowed His priesthood, and performed unrecordable miracles (see 3 Nephi 11–28). I imagine sitting and watching every moment of it in perfect bliss and a state of wonder that only comes from witnessing God's Son.

But one thing He said would cause my body to surge with the call to action: "Have ye any that are sick among you? Bring them hither. Have ye any that are lame, or blind, or halt, or maimed, or leprous, or that are withered, or that are deaf, or that are afflicted in any manner? Bring them hither and I will heal them, for I have compassion upon you; my bowels are filled with mercy" (3 Nephi 17:7). I can see it. I would hurry to gather my sweet little son Zane in my arms. This was who I was waiting for: the Christ who heals.

I imagine carrying my son's cuddly, petite frame one step after the other, up the temple's path to meet the Savior, his curly black hair tickling my cheek and his innocent giggle bringing a bounce to my step and a warmth to my spirit. The path might be rocky, and at times I might stumble and fall, but I would keep going with my eyes focused on Christ.

Sweat would bead my brow and my muscles would probably grow weak and achy, but I would still climb forward and upward, and we would get closer and closer. I can almost hear the words He spoke off in the distance as He took each person, one by one, and healed them.

Finally, I would arrive.

It is then that I would look into my Savior's eyes and place my world into His arms. I can feel my eyes plead with His—please make my son's body whole. Please, bless his ears that they hear clearly, his eyes that they see without pain, his muscles that they may be strong enough to hold him up, his lungs that they may carry the breath necessary for life, his heart that it might be free from defect, and his voice that he may speak. But, please, Jesus, don't change his soul. Keep his spirit. Keep the Down syndrome. Keep what makes him Zane. I don't think I would say a word; I just know that Christ would know a mother's heart through the plea in her eyes.

Then He would bless him and heal him. My son would be made perfect before me, all because of a loving God who sacrificed His Son.

My tears would wash the feet of my Savior as I knelt in humble and overwhelming gratitude for His sacrifice for my boy. But then, to my surprise and astonishment, Christ would reach down, place His hands on my head, and He would heal me. He would heal my anxiety, my weaknesses, and my shortcomings. He would erase my doubts and calm my troubled heart. Christ would not send me away broken. Christ would leave me perfectly whole.

You see, the path to Him would not have been easy; I probably would have hit bumps and trials along the way, but somehow I know I would have forgotten my own afflictions as I carried my Zane to meet his Savior.

It is in that moment, as I read the account in 3 Nephi, that I begin to understand the words of President Henry B. Eyring: "By helping others come unto Him, you will find that you have come unto Him yourself" ("Come unto Christ," *Ensign*, Mar. 2008).

That is what this gospel is about. That is the point. We must bring others to Christ, and by so doing, we too may know Him.

I realize now that when I see myself in the scriptures, I do not see myself as Mary next to the manger, or as Mary Magdalene at the tomb. I am in the multitude; I am in His fold. My name wouldn't even be written on the pages of the story; people would likely pass by any account of my presence. But my contribution would still matter to God.

In every scripture story, the small things become great things through Jesus Christ. The nameless disciples are beloved disciples and followers of Christ, just like the scripture heroes we name and remember.

They are the members of the multitude that carry their afflicted to the feet of the Savior, forgetting their own needs. They are the wives of men on journeys to the promised land, staying focused on their testimonies of Christ. They are "the one" who escaped to help Lot or the "three hundred and eighteen" who were ready to rescue and allow Jesus to save.

The unnamed disciples we pass right by are the faithful who prayed for Alma the Younger, or those who received their brethren after hearing their stories. A quiet heroine is a queen who stood by her fallen king. Daily disciples in the scriptures carry the bed of their brethren through a hole in the roof to Jesus, and they are in-tune instruments in the hands of the Lord, allowing Him to send earthly angels to bless His children.

Faithful disciples find their place in the fold by bringing others to Christ and coming unto Him themselves.

You and I are called to serve as humble disciples under the direction of our Heavenly Father. Our names may not be recorded in manuals and record books, and some may see our stories and pass right by without a second thought. But, to the people we are sent to love and the God we are asked to follow, a life of daily discipleship will keep us on the path to return to our omnipotent Father in Heaven and His Son, Jesus Christ.

FULFILL GOD'S MISSION

I am always fascinated by the story of Lot in the book of Genesis. Lot was Abram's nephew and found himself in need of rescue. Lot lived near Sodom and Gomorrah and over time moved himself closer and closer to the wicked cities. When the battle of the kings commenced, Lot was found and captured. But "there was one that had escaped, and told Abram" (Genesis 14:13).

Hearing this, Abram, who we later learn to be Abraham, gathered up three hundred and eighteen of his best and most trained servants and even offered up his own safety to rescue Lot from the enemy. Abram's mission was successful, and he rescued Lot, his stolen goods, and the other people who had been captured (see Genesis 14:14–16). Lot was important enough to his uncle and to God that Abram sent the very strongest people to save him.

Lot did not go on to live a perfect life devoid of sin or failure; the rest of his story can be quite complicated. But his soul was important to God, it was important to Abram, and it was worth saving. For "the Lord knoweth how to deliver the godly out of temptations, and to reserve the unjust unto the day of judgment to be punished" (2 Peter 2:9).

I try to imagine myself in the story. Where would I fit, and what role would God have asked me to fill? I try to remember times I escaped temptations of evil or when I got to assist in the rescuing. I realize there are times we are like Abram, assembling armies to save the lost and wandering. Other times, we are Lot, well-meaning but lost and in need of rescue.

Sometimes, we are the "one that had escaped, and told Abram." I really love this "one," because this person had the courage not only to find refuge for her or himself but to use that freedom to go forward and lay the foundation for Lot's rescue. This individual didn't know the outcome to the story. He or she didn't know whether Abram would hear the pleas, if Lot would be saved, or if they both would be captured and punished. But this "one" proceeded forward anyway. Somebody heard of a man in need of a rescue, and that person sought the help needed to carry out that rescue.

I can imagine running through the tall weeds until my lungs burned, hiding behind trees and scrub brush with my heart pounding so hard I could feel it in every part of me. I can picture finally getting to Abram and sharing the story with so much urgency that it wouldn't make any sense, and I would have to try again. It would be scary to be this "one." I think my eyes would fill up with tears and I would collapse against the wall in relieved exhaustion when I saw the armies assembling and knew my friend would be saved.

I think most often, though, we are among the three hundred and eighteen of Abram's servants, being born and raised under the tutelage of our Heavenly Father, becoming strong in the truth, waiting to be called up to the front lines to save and preserve God's children unto Him. Being brought up in Abram's house, they may have awoken every day and done what they knew to be right without ever knowing whether their efforts would be needed. They might have built their muscles and testimonies, practiced their approach, and been ready to act the moment they were called upon. Then, they would go forward when asked, unaware of the outcome but willing to give their lives to save the lost if it were necessary.

One spring a few years ago, I had the opportunity to see each of these roles fulfilled in the building of God's kingdom during what I now affectionately call "The Great Temple Tour of 2018."

My husband and I had built and moved into a new home a couple of years prior and quickly made friends with our neighbors. As the months passed, we visited across our driveways and front yards and eventually went on double dates together. Our new friends shared their stories of conversion with us, and we learned of the joy they had felt at their recent baptisms. We got to know one another's children and loved them as our own as we laughed and chatted over barbecued hot dogs and potato salad in the summers and board games and cookies in the winter.

As the anniversary of their baptisms approached, they shared with us their desire to prepare to attend the temple and be sealed. We were elated for our friends, and our couple prayers included their names on a nightly basis as we sought ways to support them in this journey and decision.

One night, at the close of our prayers, we began talking about what we could do to help. Together, we realized that our area only provided a temple preparation course for young adults preparing to serve missions. I knew the instructor of that course and he was simply amazing, but it seemed odd to suggest that our friends attend class with eighteen-year-olds when their children were almost that age themselves.

We brought this to the attention of our bishop and shared that if he would like, we would love to teach the temple preparation course to our friends in our home. The bishop took time to consider it and met with our friends to discuss their desires. A couple months later, he called to give us the all-clear to begin lessons. I was so excited! Two things you need to know about me are that I love to teach and I love the temple, so my preparations for the first lesson took over everything I did. I could not wait!

The months that followed were somewhat magical. We would get our young kids tucked in bed and then send a message to the group texting chain to tell them we were ready. We all sat around the table with our manuals and scriptures open. Everyone asked questions and we would search the materials for the answers. Sometimes our lessons would last late into the night and then we would continue the conversation by sending messages back and forth throughout the week about the new things we had learned and wanted to share during our next lesson.

The Spirit was strong in these meetings, and it became clear that our Heavenly Father was mindful not only of them, but also of us. I came to know my husband's testimony in a new way, I was able to see the Spirit speak to my friends' hearts over and over again, and I was renewed in my testimony of the sanctity of the temple and the personal, solemn commitments I made there. The funny part was, I had believed that I was praying to know how to help them, when the answer would be exactly what I needed myself.

During this time, our hearts were laden with worry for our future. My husband, Tanner, is a member of the military and had faithfully served for nine years at the time. We had learned during these lessons that he would be called away for a year of service overseas at the beginning of the summer. We had so many things we wanted to do in preparation for his departure, but between work, our children, our callings, and these beloved meetings, we had almost no time left to do anything. There were moments that I felt frustrated that I could not be two places at once or fulfill every role as perfectly as I wanted to.

But the Lord knew better. He allowed us the opportunity to spend this time speaking about the temple within the walls of our home. He gave us a unique opportunity to invite the Spirit into our hearts in a way we had not previously done, and He provided a way for us to seek and speak of the best things as a healing balm for the uncertainties we faced.

It felt like the big day we had been preparing for would never come. All four of us were so anxious for them to get the two most important signatures on the most important paper they would ever possess, certifying them as worthy temple recommend holders. They made an appointment first with the bishop and then the stake president and were found ready and worthy to attend the temple.

We sat down at our last temple preparation class with our calendars open to find the perfect date. I felt so honored that they wanted us there so much that they hoped to plan around Tanner's deployment schedule. We quickly realized that there was only one option, the first Saturday in March. They called the temple and set it up—an endowment session Friday night and their sealing the next morning. It was going to be a perfect weekend.

Days later, Tanner received a phone call from his best friend from high school, David[1]. Many years prior, Tanner's family had come to love and know this friend as they too broke bread and opened their hearts and homes to one

1. Names and identifying details in stories have been changed.

another. They had sat together in the living room and listened to missionary discussions, read the Book of Mormon, and shared testimony. Together, these families rejoiced when David's family chose to be baptized. Tanner and David became lifelong best friends.

That day on the phone, David and Tanner had fun catching up, talking about jobs and kids and wishing they could be together more often. Then David explained that he and his wife had prepared to enter the temple to be sealed to their beautiful children. David expressed that he wanted Tanner to accompany him through this sacred experience, just as he had during his baptism. Tanner was shocked but so excited! He could not imagine missing this moment in David's life. This was an answer to prayers that had been offered on David's behalf for many, many years. We were just unsure how we were going to pull it all off.

Both friends whom we dearly loved were preparing to seal and unite their families in God's holy house—on the same day. One couple in the Salt Lake Temple, the other in the Manti Utah Temple. Two couples, two endowment sessions, two sealings, in two temples that are located two hours apart, two days before a yearlong deployment.

Feverishly, we calculated and crunched numbers trying to figure out if it was possible to basically be two places at once. I wore out my Google Maps app trying to defy the odds of Utah traffic. Thankfully, it appeared that we could attend the temple with all four friends. We would attend the Friday evening endowment session with our neighbors in the Salt Lake Temple. Following that session, we would drive to Manti and wake up early for the Saturday morning endowment session with David and his wife. Immediately following that session, David's family would be sealed for time and all eternity in a quaint sealing room in the beautiful Manti temple. We would then drive back to the Salt Lake Temple to witness the sealing of our neighbors that afternoon, thus ending "The Great Temple Tour of 2018." We would then return home, pack Tanner's belongings, and prepare to say goodbye for the next year.

The plan was set.

When the busy weekend finally arrived, we began to carefully carry out each detail, and truly there were angels on our side as everything went off without a hitch.

What I saw in each of these temple sessions and sealings, however, was something I hadn't planned to see. Each couple welcomed friends and families from many years past to witness these ordinances. Longtime friends with full hearts rejoiced with them over their unions in God's temples. I watched as each couple hugged and cried with coworkers who had invited them to church years ago, sisters who had written their names on prayer rolls, and aunts, uncles, cousins, parents, and grandparents who had prayed day after day to have this moment in the temple with their loved ones.

This is to say, each of these couples had individuals in

their lives who are like "the one" spoken of in Genesis. These ones faithfully escaped moments of uncertainties in their own lives and quickly sought relief for their friends. Like the one who sought the help of Abram to rescue Lot, these ones called upon their Heavenly Father to rescue their brothers, sisters, children, and friends in the gospel. They forgot the trials of their own hearts and sought to provide refuge for those who so desperately required it, and they did it without thinking about themselves. They had no idea how the story would end or if their pleadings would be pointless, but they continued forward anyway. They probably had moments when their hearts pounded in their chests and they felt that they couldn't go on. And now, in the temple, I witnessed as they collapsed in the relief and love of their loved ones' rescue.

Also among us in the temples were the three hundred and eighteen—those who were prepared and ready to go forth when called on to perform the rescue. These are the friends, missionaries, ward members, ministering brothers and sisters, bishops, elders quorum presidents, and Relief Society presidents who followed their heavenly guide to reach out, lift, comfort, and carry these friends to the gospel. They, like the three hundred and eighteen, followed their heavenly leader through inspiration of the Holy Ghost to provide relief, teach, and allow room for Christ to save.

I think of these faithful brothers and sisters reading their scriptures daily and attending a long list of church meetings week after week. They had spent their entire lives in preparation to assist in bringing souls to Christ, striving to always be ready to act when called upon. Those endowment and sealing rooms were filled with people who acted and loved in spectacular ways.

Most importantly, though, like the one and the three hundred and eighteen, they set out to do all of this to save one soul. They invited one friend to church. They prayed for their one son or daughter. They took treats and ministering messages to one sister. They sat by one man in priesthood meeting. They looked for and found the one who needed to be found. In return, the Lord received their efforts and magnified them. One man sealed to one woman united generations, just as the mission to rescue Lot also saved those who were with him (see Genesis 14:16).

As we serve like the one pleading to God for relief for our loved ones or prepare faithfully and stand ready to act when called upon like the three hundred and eighteen, we are standing in places that allow us to fulfill the missions God has prepared for us. This faithful willingness and preparation will allow us to be in the places we are needed, reach the people He has prepared for us to reach, and serve the missions He has called us to serve. Being an everyday disciple is being prepared to act when God calls.

President M. Russell Ballard taught: "Member missionary work does not require strategies or gimmicks. It does require faith—real faith and trust in the Lord. It also requires genuine love" ("The Essential Role of Member Missionary Work," *Ensign*, May 2003). Often, it is easy to complicate our call to serve as member missionaries. We can feel inadequate or even pushy. But, like the unnamed heroes in Genesis, we can move forward with faith and love to accomplish the work of God.

I pondered this lesson in those temples, knowing my husband and I had been called to a much different mission in the days to follow. My mind raced with the things we needed to get done before he left and the activities we should have completed with our kids. Then the Spirit gently reminded me that we had prepared and were sitting in the place He needed us to sit, at the time He needed us to be there, with the people He had called us to serve. God had allowed us to be one of the three hundred and eighteen.

Tanner left the next day, and the burden of the mission weighed heavily on my heart. He spent the weeks that followed in preparation for the deployment with his unit on a local base. Then, almost out of nowhere, his call was canceled, he returned home, and his mission was changed. We have little explanation as to why this was the case; there was paperwork filed incorrectly and a quota that was met without him. Regardless of the reason, to me, it was truly a miracle. A miracle because the Lord was preparing us to carry other burdens.

Again, the Spirit whispered that we were in the place He had called us to be, with the people He needed us to be with, learning the lessons and serving the missions He had called us to serve. As a result, we repeatedly saw the miracles that came from daily disciples who pleaded to Heavenly Father like "the one" and who stood ready to serve, like the three hundred and eighteen, while we found ourselves feeling as though it were our turn to be Lot, in need of respite and rescue, because "the Lord knoweth how to deliver the godly" (2 Peter 2:9).

As you seek to stand firm and serve the Lord every day, do not become discouraged or overwhelmed believing that only grand gestures are needed in building the kingdom. Your efforts to look for and serve people one by one are actions that lead each of us to become more like the Savior.

You have already been somebody's "one" and you've been in another's army of three hundred and eighteen, even if the story remains unwritten or seemingly forgotten. You are already serving as a quiet hero every day when you cry out to the Lord for your loved ones and as you dedicate your life to be ready to serve all who feel lost in the world but are lovingly remembered by God. You are a needed disciple because you stand ready to assist in the rescue.

TRUST GOD THROUGH THE JOURNEY

In the book of 1 Nephi in the Book of Mormon, we are introduced to the prophet Lehi, his faithful son Nephi, and their life in Jerusalem. The entire book is action-packed; it definitely gets the reader hooked on the first page! Nephi writes about his father's prophecies of the destruction of Jerusalem, the wickedness of the people, and the family's eventual descent into the wilderness and journey to a promised land.

We read stories of resilience and heroism as Nephi, Laman, Lemuel, and Sam return to Jerusalem to obtain the brass plates. The men experience success after several failed attempts when Nephi courageously follows promptings to kill the wicked Laban. Nephi talks about bringing Zoram, the servant of Laban, with him out of Jerusalem and later returns to bring Ishmael, his wife, and their children on their journey. We mourn with Nephi over his broken bow repaired through inspiration, and we watch as a boat is built line upon line until it is ready to carry the family to the land the Lord had prepared. We sing about these stories in Primary classes and strive to be like Nephi—courageous and willing to do anything the Lord commands with the faith to know He will prepare the way (see 1 Nephi 3:7).

For many of us, the story of Nephi, Lehi, and their family members lays the foundation for our testimony of the scriptures. There is no doubt that Nephi loved the Lord and was a true disciple and righteous follower of Christ.

But just as there is much to learn from the faithfulness of Nephi, I love to think about the devotion of the quiet, lesser-known disciples in his family. In 1 Nephi 7, the Lord inspired Lehi to have Nephi and his brothers return to Jerusalem to invite the house of Ishmael to join them on their journey. They taught Ishmael the things of the Lord, and the Lord softened Ishmael's heart. It seems Ishmael and his family had come to know for themselves, through the Spirit of the Lord, that the things Nephi and his brothers taught were true and had the faith to act on this newly strengthened testimony.

Think about what that would look like for a moment. Ishmael and his family were in Jerusalem, working and living out everyday life. We do not know the details of their thoughts and hearts, but it is possible that they had not previously seen a need to journey or leave their home. In fact, I wonder if they were completely content. Then, the sons of a man who had preached of Christ and the destruction of their city showed up at their door and taught them incredible truths. In what to us seems like no time at all, they were packing up to leave everything they knew and all their worldly possessions behind to follow promptings by the Spirit and trust in the word of Nephi and his brothers.

I don't know if they knew Lehi's family before this day, but if they didn't, Ishmael agreed to leave everything they had, all they knew, and their entire lives to follow strangers. That is a level of conviction to follow the Spirit I can only hope to have.

Not long into their journey, two of Ishmael's daughters, two of his sons, their families, Laman, and Lemuel rebelled against Nephi and sought to return to Jerusalem. They even tied him up and spoke unkindly. Relying on his faith in his father and not wanting his loved ones to be destroyed, Nephi called upon God to grant him the power to overcome those in rebellion and offered them his forgiveness. The families then continued their journey and arrived at the tent of Lehi (see 1 Nephi 7:6–22).

In the scriptures, it sounds like their journey to Lehi's tent was short. In reality, I think it had to have been rough. Have you ever walked into a room where people have been in an argument? The air is heavy and you can literally feel the anger between the people. I usually laugh nervously and dart my eyes around the room, hoping for a way out. Now imagine that same feeling, with no escape plan, sand stuck to your face, and a rock stuck in your sandals. I can only imagine that it must have been a long walk.

It isn't like they arrived at Lehi's tent and all was well then, either. This rebellion was not an isolated incident—frustrations and disputations were a recurring part of their journey. The sons of Lehi married the daughters of Ishmael and they continued toward the promised land.

I often wonder how Ishmael and his wife, who I will affectionately call "Sister Ishmael," must have felt. They had come to know the truthfulness of this prophet for themselves and felt propelled to act. They were willing to give up everything to follow the path of truth and brought their children along for the journey. I would imagine they felt joy as one of their beloved daughters joined hands in marital unity with Nephi—excited to see her learn of the truth for herself and unite that testimony with a righteous son of God. Similar emotions likely followed when other equally beloved daughters married Zoram and Sam.

I like to think that the marriages of their daughters to Laman and Lemuel were joyous as well. I wonder if faithful anticipation filled the air as these parents could see the potential and greatness in these men and prayed that the union would result in eternal righteousness. I believe they hoped that these unions would be a credit and a blessing to their families for generations.

As the journey continued, both faithfulness and rebellion prevailed in both families. As Nephi and others continued to strengthen their resolve to follow a plan outlined by a loving Heavenly Father, Laman, Lemuel, and their wives questioned the motives and intentions of Nephi and ultimately, the Lord.

I cannot help but think about Brother and Sister Ishmael in all of this. There they were, in the middle of nowhere because they believed the messages they had been taught in Jerusalem. Some of their children appeared to have heeded the call, while others succumbed to the beguiling influence of their friends and spouses. I would imagine that their prayers every night included the names of each child, as any parent's might. Praying for all of them, regardless of their circumstance, to be carried by the light of Christ through their hardships.

Then, in the middle of it all, Ishmael died (see 1 Nephi 16:34). He died before reaching the promised land. He likely died before seeing all his prayers answered. He died before knowing the fruits of his sacrifice, and maybe, he died in heartache for children who were struggling in faith. Sister Ishmael was left to carry on, likely devastated and still heavily laden with the troubles of a mother's and now a widow's heart.

We cannot read this story without seeing that these disciples of Christ truly are incredible. Their faith and devotion did not give way to great fanfare. These parents likely had burdens that felt quite heavy.

There is so much we do not know, but what we do know teaches a profound lesson. These unsung disciples pressed forward with faith in the Lord and His prophet regardless of the trials swirling around them. Through their willingness to humbly obey while trusting in God, we can see that faithful progression through the wildernesses of life leads us to a greater knowledge of Him.

I wonder what may have happened if we had more of Brother and Sister Ishmael's story recorded. Maybe we would have missed seeing the miracles God provided for those families, focusing instead on the seemingly unanswered desires. They moved forward, step by step, allowing the Lord and His goodness, through revelation to His prophets, to be the hero in the story of Nephi, all alongside unnamed disciples who lovingly obeyed their prophet and their God, regardless of their afflictions.

This reminds me of my wise friends John and Ashley.

John and Ashley, although living a country apart, grew up in families that lived, loved, and taught the gospel. They both had many siblings, lived in rural communities, and worked hard from sunup to sundown, with lots of moments for love and laughter in between. From young ages, they developed their own testimonies as they attended church meetings with their families and immersed themselves in their Young Men and Young Women quorums and classes.

John served an honorable mission and learned to love the Lord with all his heart. He served in Alabama, where the air was heavy and wet. He remembers riding a bike through the hot, humid air and feeling as though he were riding through a steam room. He would carry a rag in his backpack to wipe his brow before knocking on doors, only to have them slammed in his face. Every once in a while a door would open all the way, and this is when John would shine. He loved teaching the gospel and had a magnetic personality. Everyone who talked to him absolutely loved him, and they soon loved the gospel just as much. John decided that his mission was never going to end when he got home. He had a fire that could not be stopped.

Ashley graduated from high school and left home to begin her studies at college. She is one of those people who seem to have every talent. She can cook anything from scratch and have it taste like it came from a five-star restaurant, while singing like an angel. Then, she could cut and style your hair, sew you a dress, and make you a corsage before sending you out the door for prom. She would sit up and wait for you while she prepared one of the best Relief Society lessons you had ever heard, full of scripture references and perfectly worded questions. The best part is that she is also the humblest sister you'll ever meet. She can do all of this without a soul knowing, which is what she prefers, and perhaps it is what sets her apart.

When John completed his mission, he became a student at the same college Ashley was attending. Soon their paths crossed, and before long, John knew he was head over heels in love. He knew she was the one when they spent an entire day decorating the church cultural hall for a single adult dance. He held the ladder as she insisted on climbing up and down to hang each ribbon perfectly. She was fearless and beautiful, and he was smitten.

The two soon married in the temple and started a family, with the hopes of raising their children in truth and light as their parents had faithfully done. Growing a family was difficult for them. It took years before they learned they were expecting their first child. They were so excited when they finally received the news. They called their parents and friends, who rejoiced with them. They prepared the nursery and Ashley sewed little blankets and onesies.

As Ashley's due date approached, the growing and movement in her belly decreased. Her mother's heart knew something was wrong. She called her doctor, who told her not to worry. She asked John for a blessing. He laid his hands upon her head, but the words they both wanted, the promise of perfect healing, never came.

That night, Ashley held her tiny, perfect, stillborn baby in her arms while sitting on her bedroom floor, leaning against the side of her bed as she sobbed. She thought she would never be the same. She would never forget her angel baby.

Months later, Ashley found she was expecting another child, who came into the world perfectly healthy. She doted on his every movement and cuddled him close at every opportunity. Over the years, Ashley had six children to raise on this earth and three who returned home before their first breath of life. Each loss embedded in her and John not only a desire but a desperate need to build a family that would last into the eternities. They hungered after the promise of forever.

As their children grew, so did their efforts to teach them the gospel. They attended church meetings as a family and knelt in prayer together morning and night. Careful planning and attention were given to family home evening lessons, with the intention to invite the Spirit and strengthen family bonds. They spent many nights roasting marshmallows together and playing card games.

When their kids were teenagers, their house became the hangout for the neighborhood. They always had an open-door policy with kids coming and going. It felt like the kitchen was a twenty-four-hour diner. Someone was always concocting a snack, and John was often up talking with the kids about anything you could imagine. Walking into their front door was like walking into a hug. On Sunday evenings, there were sometimes twenty people there for dinner and the whole house was filled with laughter.

Both parents woke early each morning to prepare breakfast, and they read from the scriptures together as a family. Their son laughs and says that when he would get on the bus, the other kids would always tease him for making them hungry since he smelled of bacon and eggs.

As their children aged, they began to have their own experiences. Some made friendships with individuals who called their faith into question. John and Ashley did everything they could to teach and redirect. One child attended a youth camp. The whole time he was gone, his parents prayerfully pleaded that he would feel the Spirit just enough to try a little harder. Instead, he came home and told them he was certain God did not exist.

Ashley said there aren't words in the dictionary to describe how it felt to have her child denounce her Heavenly Father and Redeemer. She tried to keep going as normal, but a piece of her heart died with her son's faith. She lost count of the nights spent crying herself to sleep while offering a never-ending prayer.

One by one, more of their children came to the same conclusion. They would have the same talk over and over and encourage each child to try a little longer to hold on to faith. Nothing seemed to work. Their prayers felt like they fell on deaf ears, their fasts seemed to be fruitless, and their tear-stained pillows seemed to never dry as night after night, they lay awake wetting them once again.

John and Ashley decided that they must have failed.

Their prayers continued on behalf of their children, but as one year turned to five, then five to ten and ten to fifteen, they began to feel as though their children were lost in darkness. They were certain that they would not be found in this life and focused their efforts on praying for their hope in the next.

On one occasion John remarked: "I don't know where I went wrong. I play it over and over in my mind. Regardless of my efforts, my children are lost and will probably never return. The hardest part is knowing that they face hardships that Heavenly Father so desperately wants to help them with. All they have to do is reach out."

John and Ashley continued in faith along the journey God had for them. They devoted their lives to obedience and often felt a renewed sense of ability to increase their faith in God and His ability to reach their children. When they continued forward, faithfully carrying the burdens placed upon their shoulders, the heaviness decreased as their love for their fellow men continued to take the forefront in the narrative of their lives. They began to see the Savior's goodness more fully and to understand His love more deeply.

When I think of John and Ashley's heartache as they watch their children struggle and wade through adversity, my mind turns back to Brother and Sister Ishmael, pressing on in what they believed to be right while adversity swirled around them.

Brother and Sister Ishmael never fully saw the whole story while in this life; they would pass on before ever knowing all that their posterity would be known for. They didn't see that throughout the years and generations, their children, grandchildren, and beyond would be known as righteous followers at times and would struggle in faith and delight in wickedness at others. Surely the multitude that knelt at the Savior's feet as a testimony of His Resurrection as recorded in 3 Nephi likely included members of their beloved posterity. They didn't know it, but miracles beyond imagination came from their sacrifices.

Nephi learned that their journey in the wilderness was so much more than a trip to a new place. The Lord said to Nephi: "After ye have arrived in the promised land, ye shall know that I, the Lord, am God; and that I, the Lord, did deliver you from destruction; yea, that I did bring you out of the land of Jerusalem" (1 Nephi 17:14).

Like Nephi, Ishmael and his wife were saved through the Lord from destruction in Jerusalem and were given a journey to embark on. That journey was fraught with challenges that through faithfulness would become the very instances that would testify to them that "I, the Lord, am God." They too were saved through the Savior and chosen in the furnace of their afflictions (see 1 Nephi 20:10). They were refined through adversity and strengthened in trial.

President Russell M. Nelson taught: "My dear brothers and sisters, the joy we feel has little to do with the circumstances of our lives and everything to do with the focus of our lives" ("Joy and Spiritual Survival," *Ensign*, Nov. 2016).

For Brother and Sister Ishmael, John and Ashley, and all of us, the ability and desire to focus on the great things of God is paramount in finding joy in the journey out of destruction and to the promised land. Even greater, though, is the joy that appears from coming to know the Savior through the afflictions presented along the path and allowing Him to be "the light that shineth in darkness" (Doctrine and Covenants 45:7).

Elder Dieter F. Uchtdorf invites us to embark on the journey. He says: "Come and see what this marvelous, wondrous, and adventurous journey is all about. Along the way you will discover yourself. You will discover meaning. You will discover God. You will discover the most adventurous and glorious journey of your life" ("Your Great Adventure," *Ensign*, Nov. 2019).

Often, we will not know the end of the journey or see our efforts fully come to fruition. But when we place our faith and confidence in the Lord's plan and timing, we can move forward knowing He will make greatness out of all things. By embarking on the journey, we can come to Him. When trials seem to swirl around us and the journey feels long and difficult, we can either see the Lord in the steps that lead to redemption or turn from Him, finding loneliness and solitude. Sometimes being a disciple of Christ means simply being willing to stay amongst His sheep, standing as close to the Master as we can.

Every time you keep moving forward, following the prophets and the word of the Lord amidst heartache and trial, you are living the life of a humble disciple. You do not know how your story will unfold. You do not know the fullness of the plan the Father has for you and your posterity. But still, you keep trying, keep praying, and you stand faithful, and that is truly heroic.

LEARN ONE ANOTHER'S STORIES

In the book of Mosiah, King Mosiah is leading the righteous in the land of Zarahemla. During this time, there are Saints across the land seeking the refuge Zarahemla offered to followers of Christ.

One of these groups was the people of Alma. These faithful Saints fled from the reign of the wicked King Noah and sought refuge in the wilderness. They had become converted and been baptized before embarking on a journey toward Zarahemla to live amongst Mosiah's people. Their journey had been trying and difficult, as the people of the king were angry with them and with Alma for leaving their place in the kingdom. They faced persecution and were at times burdened by taskmasters, but eventually, they were led to find the land of Zarahemla and entered the peace found therein because of the goodness and mercy of God (see Mosiah 24).

The people of Limhi also sought refuge at this time. They were under the rule of the Lamanites because of the wickedness of their forefathers, and they desperately desired relief. They had fought in wars and failed to be victorious. They even sent men to find Zarahemla but instead found the records that we now know to be the book of Ether. Though these records are a needed and sacred blessing, the total freedom and relief they so desperately desired remained unrealized.

Eventually, Ammon found them and testified of God, proving that he was indeed a friend aiding in their deliverance, not the foe they thought they were encountering. He led them out the back gates when the guards were drunk and took them to the land of Zarahemla (see Mosiah 17–22).

It is a lot to take in, but Zarahemla was probably getting pretty full and busy by now. They had refugees coming from all over the place. We don't have to look far in our own towns and countries to see that sometimes it is difficult for people to welcome refugees into their homes. In fact, sometimes they reject and torment them. But Mosiah "received them with joy" (Mosiah 22:14). Every single one of them.

I wonder if King Mosiah feared that his people would be less joyful than he was, because he took immediate action to create unity. Upon the arrival of all these people from different lands, understandings, and backgrounds, he read their stories. He gathered the people, both old and new, and read the stories of Alma and Limhi's people. He shared their accounts of when their ancestors left Zarahemla and of their return. He spoke of their trials and victories, how the Lord had succored them, and how they had overcome so much to be able to arrive in Zarahemla at that time.

I imagine it being like a big general conference with everyone sitting shoulder to shoulder—the refugees next to the people who had lived there a long time. I wonder if tears rolled down their cheeks when Mosiah read the part specifically about them and they remembered feeling so lost. When he got to their war chapters, I wonder if their hearts broke when they remembered their fathers, brothers, or friends who had fought and died. I love to picture them looking around the multitude at one another as each story was told, realizing Mosiah was not talking about strangers; he was teaching about the brothers and sisters they were sitting beside. Maybe hugs were offered and received and a safety was felt that some in the multitude had never felt before.

"And now, when Mosiah had made an end of reading the records, his people who tarried in the land were struck with wonder and amazement. For they knew not what to think; for when they beheld those that had been delivered out of bondage they were filled with exceedingly great joy" (Mosiah 25:7–8).

Joy. All it took was coming to know their stories, and they were filled with "exceedingly great joy." When we take the time to know one another, to truly know each other's stories and backgrounds, we are prepared to experience the joy that comes from understanding and unity.

Sister Marjorie Pay Hinckley is one of my favorite

examples. She was such a light. She shared: "People are wonderful. Each one has a story, each something to give, each knows something interesting, something that can make your life richer" (*Small and Simple Things* [Salt Lake City: Deseret Book, 2003], 134).

King Mosiah's people seemed to know and understand this. I think they knew that by coming to hear and know the stories of their fellow brothers and sisters in the gospel, they would learn what those around them had to give, and in turn, their own lives would be enriched through knowing these people's stories. Placing myself in the shoes of Alma and Limhi's people, I would imagine they considered these Saints to be like everyday heroes for their willingness to learn about and accept them as they were, and truly each of these brave congregation members had found their place.

From the moment our Heavenly Father created the heavens and the earth, He has caused there to be a record kept, beginning with the book of Genesis. These sacred records teach us about His ways and goodness. They instill in us a desire to learn more about His prophets from long ago and connect our hearts to those whose stories are recorded. Throughout the Restoration, Joseph Smith and other early prophets recorded the stories of the Saints and the guidance they received from the Lord in the Doctrine and Covenants, and in present day, the words and stories of the gospel continue to be preserved and recorded. Our prophets also urge us to keep records of our own lives and the Lord's presence in them. I can only imagine that these records are kept for many wise purposes—most we do not yet know (see 1 Nephi 9:5)—but I often wonder if one of those purposes is to connect the hearts of the children of God as we seek to hear, read, and understand one another's stories, backgrounds, and testimonies.

Have you ever met someone and had a less than desirable first impression? Maybe that person was rude, quiet, or very boisterous the first time you met, and you were unsure what to think of it? I know I have had that experience.

During high school, I worked in a small copy store and post office in a tiny town. Customers would come in at all hours of the day, make copies, send important documents, and shop for scrapbooking paper. Because our town was so small, often we would have only one customer in the store at a time. This allowed for many opportunities to visit with and really get to know them. We were not open very long before we knew the names of all the customers, their copy and shipping preferences, and usually a few details about their lives.

I had a customer who told me stories about growing up in New York City, riding the subway to school and coming home before the streetlights turned on. I had customers who shared about the businesses they were growing and their dreams for the future. We saw customers who were dedicated Primary teachers who came in to make handouts, booklets, and gifts for their beloved Primary children.

Sometimes, the first impressions of these customers were wonderful. They offered warm smiles and friendly greetings as they entered the store. Others were harsher, more frustrated, and far less easy to work with. Often, after speaking more with them and helping to provide the service they had come to receive, we would learn about a burden pressing upon their heart at the time. Then it became very easy to forgive the initial harshness of their behavior.

On one such occasion, a young mother entered the store. Her demeanor was somber and withdrawn. Her eyes were red and blotchy, and she could barely whisper as she spoke. I remember leaning across the counter to get close enough to hear her. She slid a piece of paper over to me and asked for the best copies on the best paper. I looked down and saw a picture of a perfect baby boy. His smile spread across the page and his sweet innocence brightened my heart. Below the photo, a recent birth date was written in ornate script, followed by a dash and another date I realized had been only two days prior. A death date.

My eyes locked with this loving mother's and we just cried.

As I made her copies, she shared her story with me. She talked about her precious son and the events that had led up to his return to his Father in Heaven. Hers was a burden I could not lift; I was qualified only to make the best and most important photocopies I had ever made, but I could also listen to her story. I was honored to listen to and cry alongside this devastated sister. I do not know her name; I do not know the story that came before that day or her story that followed. What I do know is that by hearing her and taking the time to feel her heart, I felt a desire to pray for and have never forgotten this customer. Truly, this sister and her story left me "struck with wonder and amazement" (Mosiah 25:7–8).

When I became a foster parent, one of my biggest fears was that I would struggle to have patience and compassion for the parents of the children placed in my care. I could not see how I could care for someone who had potentially neglected a child.

Each child who entered our home arrived with a purple binder. Inside were pages filled with stories. I learned about parents who had experienced abuse, neglect, torture, loss of children, and other horrifically traumatizing events. As I read these pages, my heart filled with love and compassion toward them. I came to know that many of them were raised similarly to me but experienced trials that made it nearly impossible for them to function. When I made an effort to come to know these people, God placed within me the ability to see them as He saw them and love them more like He loved them, and once again, I was "struck with wonder and amazement."

I have known my husband and his family since I was eleven years old. We were in the same ward and spent much of our youth together as our families became fast friends.

One of the benefits to knowing my husband this long is that I have also known his siblings since they were incredibly young. In fact, I have known his younger sisters since they were nine and three years old, and I waited in the hospital hallway for his youngest sister to be born. Having no sisters of my own, these girls became my sisters long before I married their brother.

His middle sister, Rylee, was best friends with my three-year-old brother, Hunter. Their friendship, one that has continued into adulthood, allowed me to spend a lot of time with Rylee as a child.

She was always busy and doing things. I do not think she ever sat down! I remember brushing her long, blonde hair after a day at the lake, and I can hear her cute giggle when she would set up pranks around the house and wait to see me get trapped in her ridiculous schemes.

As Rylee grew, I would cheer for her at softball games and take pictures of her at prom. When our first son was born, it was fun to see her become an aunt. She would tell us about friends and schoolwork when she came over to babysit our kids, have barbecues, or watch movies in the basement. There is no doubt this world is much better because we have our Ry.

Ry always had lots of friends, but she very rarely brought them to family get-togethers. When she is with her family, she is focused and "all in." So, when she brought a friend to Christmas Eve dinner, we all quickly knew this friend was special to her. She walked her over to the buffet and showed her all the dinner options. She attended to her needs and sat near to make sure her friend was comfortable. She watched her closely, and there was definitely a twinkle in her eye and a smile on her face I certainly hadn't seen before.

In my heart, I knew this friend was someone Rylee really cared for. So, I prayed a lot. I prayed about Rylee and the things she was facing. I hoped to seek understanding of the interactions I had witnessed at Christmas Eve dinner. Over time, I felt it was likely this friend was much more than just a friend and was actually her partner.

Often, as I thought about Rylee, tears would come. My heart was broken for my sister who had likely felt alone for so long. I could not imagine the things she must have thought and felt in her Young Women and Sunday School classes. My mind reflected on the years of anxiety she had likely endured and the many offered dates she had missed, opting to stay home instead. I thought about all of our memories, and my heart could not handle the thought that she might possibly feel unwanted or unwelcome in my life and home because of our differences.

I remember sharing these concerns with my husband, Tanner, day after day. I could not shake the feeling that I just needed her to know I saw her, and I loved her. She needed to know that she and the people she loved were welcome in my life, in my heart, and in my family. I needed Rylee to know that she is and would always be my sister.

On a cold January day, I texted her. I told her I sensed that her friendship was more than most friendships she'd had in the past, and whether this was true or not, I loved her. I told her she was my sister, the aunt to my children, and a friend. I didn't want to lose her or have her feel unwanted or unwelcome for any reason. I told her if I was wrong in my impression, I was sorry for overstepping, but I wanted her to know that above all else, she was loved.

It wasn't too long after that that I got a text from my brother, Hunter. Rylee had come out to her older sister Kinzi and Hunter many, many months before she'd arrived at Christmas Eve dinner, and they had kept the dealings of her heart private as she had requested. When I texted her, she forwarded the message to both Kinzi and Hunter.

Hunter told me that Rylee had said that she was the most afraid to come out to me. She wasn't afraid to tell the rest of her siblings or parents, and she wasn't afraid to tell friends, but she was afraid to tell me. She was worried she would let me down or would be withheld from our lives.

That was one of the most heart-wrenching things I had ever heard. Tears still well up in my eyes when I think about it. The bubbly, bouncy, blonde-headed girl I loved so dearly thought I would abandon her. My actions had somehow indicated over the years that I would choose appearances over family and biases over my love for her. I am ashamed that there was ever a day I carried myself in such a way.

I believe the inspiration to send the text message that

day was not coincidence. I believe it was an effort to express that I saw her, and while I understood only a portion of her story at that time, I desired to know and understand so much more.

A couple years have passed since that Christmas Eve, and I have often thought about Rylee's life during that time. Since sharing her heart with her family, she has come out to friends and parents of friends who have known her as long as or longer than I have. She has sought employment, gotten her own apartment, purchased vehicles, and lived out in the world in her day-to-day life. When I think about judgments that have possibly come her way through all of this, I want to burst. I want to tell everyone about the Rylee I know and love! I want them to know how funny she is and that she is a wonderful aunt and loyal friend and sister. I want them to know how hard she works and how perfectly pure her love is for her family and friends. I want people to see her. I want people to know her. I want people to hear her story. I wonder if she ever wishes to just be seen.

I think that others would feel joy and be "struck with wonder and amazement" as they learned to see the sister, friend, and daughter we see. Maybe they would be slower to judge and more able to offer Christlike love if they took the time to learn about Rylee and all the things that make up who she is—her humor, kindness, and loyalty. There is so much more to every child of God than the things we see when we first meet. This is why it is so important to take the time to truly see one another and learn each other's stories.

"See me." It seems to be the plea of the hearts of so many in the world today. Our brothers and sisters are pleading with us to see them. They ask us to see beyond outward appearance. See beyond careers. See beyond intimate relationships and orientations.

As a multiracial sister in the gospel, this has often been the cry in my heart, too. When I was a child, I was the only one in my congregation who was a different ethnicity. I cried as I prayed to understand why I was different. I feared that my skin color would hold me back from entrance into heaven or other good gifts. When people would say, "I don't see color," I thought that meant they didn't see color because people of color were not worth seeing.

I prayed that others would see my heart. See my worth. See my efforts. See my work. See my soul.

Why do our hearts ache to be seen so deeply that many cry out in acts of desperation, destruction, or pain? Perhaps it is because our very spirits and beings were made by the One who sees all. We are created by a God who sees us, who hears us, who knows us perfectly.

It is the very nature of our beings to desire to be seen and to be loved exactly how we are. We left a premortal world where we were accustomed to being loved and seen. We lived and loved in the presence of One who sees and loves perfectly. It is no wonder, then, that when we feel unloved and unseen by our brothers and sisters, our souls just cannot handle the heartbreak.

Knowing this of our eternal nature, our Heavenly Father has asked us to covenant with Him to see His children as He does.

In the October 2018 general conference, Elder Robert C. Gay taught: "To take upon ourselves the name of Christ means we faithfully strive to see as God sees. How does God see? Joseph Smith said, 'While one portion of the human race is judging and condemning the other without mercy, the Great Parent of the universe looks upon the whole of the human family with a fatherly care and paternal regard,' for 'His love [is] unfathomable'" ("Taking upon Ourselves the Name of Jesus Christ," *Ensign*, Nov. 2018).

What a sacred opportunity we have been given to fulfill our promises made at baptism to take upon us the name of Christ—an opportunity to see as God sees. To love as God loves.

The true show of Christlike love and humanity comes with what we do after we see one another's differences.

I think of the parable of the good Samaritan, as recorded in Luke 10:30–37. A certain man came down from Jerusalem to Jericho and was beaten and left for dead. He was passed by both a priest and Levite, but the Samaritan stopped and saved him.

President M. Russell Ballard once said: "Have you ever wondered why the Savior chose to make the hero of this story a Samaritan? There was considerable antipathy between the Jews and the Samaritans at the time of Christ. Under normal circumstances, these two groups avoided each other. . . . His deliberate use of Jews and Samaritans clearly teaches that we are all neighbors and that we should love, esteem, respect, and serve one another despite our deepest differences—including religious, political, and cultural differences" ("Doctrine of Inclusion," *Ensign*, Nov. 2001).

To me, the miracle wasn't that the Samaritan did not see or notice that this man was a Jew. I believe the miracle came *because* he saw the Jewish man and loved him for who he was—or better still, for what he was: a son of God.

In our families, wards, and communities, the miracles will come not when we seek to be colorblind or to look past the details of others that make up who they are. The miracles of joy and unity will come when we see each other—black, white, male, female, infirm in body, differently abled or oriented—and we love like Christ.

Let us teach our children to see each color, race, and background. To celebrate it. To honor it, and to love the person enfolded therein—the child of God. For it is by truly seeing that the miracles come.

I believe we serve as everyday disciples as we look around and truly take the time to see and know the Shepherd's other sheep. If we truly know them and their stories, we can notice when they become lost, reach them when they feel alone, and encourage them to stay close to our Master. To me, a hero is someone who takes the time to know, see, and learn the stories of my loved ones so they can love them, too. I think the same is true for our Father in Heaven. I believe that to Him, His disciples take the time to know, see, and learn the stories of each of His children so that they can love as He loves.

I have seen you out there listening. I have read your insightful social media posts. I have watched you embrace your children and friends of differing orientations. I have heard you share and retell stories that bring unity. Your efforts have left me filled with wonder and amazement. You serve as a disciple of Christ with every new insight you gain and every time you truly hear and see one of your brothers or sisters in the gospel.

You are already doing so well. Keep listening. You might be somebody's quiet, listening hero.

PRAY FOR THEIR ENEMIES

The book of Mosiah continues telling the story of Alma, who went forward teaching the words of Abinadi and eventually arrived in Zarahemla.

Throughout his life, he taught of redemption, resurrection, and a Savior who would come to pay the price for sin and who would then ascend into heaven with the Father. For me, it would be easy to say that Alma traded in his previous life under the wicked King Noah for a life devoted to Christ and to his Heavenly Father.

In time, we are introduced to his son, Alma the Younger. I would imagine that based on what we know about Alma, he was an exceptional father. The passion that he applied to teaching his people about the gospel was likely magnified when he began to teach his son. I love to imagine all the Book of Mormon prophets as fathers, especially Alma. In my mind, they were remarkable.

The thing is, Alma the Younger was quite different from his father at first. Alma the Younger was a "man of many words and did speak much flattery to the people" and led many people to do iniquity (Mosiah 27:8). He began stealing the hearts of the people away from Christ and was "giving a chance for the enemy of God to exercise his power over them" (v. 9). As he and his friends went about spreading rebellion, an angel of the Lord came unto them with great power and authority—so much so that the ground shook and they arose with great astonishment.

"And now the astonishment of Alma was so great that he became dumb, that he could not open his mouth; yea and he became weak, even that he could not move his hands" (Mosiah 27:19).

Alma called the people together to see what the Lord had done for his son. If my son were struck down, I don't know if I would see it as a blessing right away, but Alma did, and he gathered everyone to see the blessing he saw.

He called upon the priests to fast and pray for Alma the Younger that he might speak and share the goodness of God with these people. These were the same priests who had led alongside Alma while his son spread destruction. They may have watched as young Alma led away their brothers and sisters in the gospel, deceived their friends, and possibly even pulled away their children and grandchildren, contributing to great unrest and uneasiness in the land. But they heeded the call and prayed anyway.

I think this would be so hard to do. For me, it would be easier to be relieved that the city's problem child was no longer a problem. It seems like there would be a lot of temptation to rejoice instead of mourn and party instead of pray.

Instead, these priests did just as the Savior teaches in 3 Nephi 12:34: "Love your enemies, bless them that curse you, do good to them that hate you, and pray for them who despitefully use you and persecute you." This truly was an act of humble discipleship.

Through their faith and sacrifice, the Lord unlocked miracles before the eyes of His children. He showed His ability to answer our cries through prayer and fasting, and the redemptive power and change of heart that occurs through the Atonement of Jesus Christ. They united in faith on Alma's behalf despite the pain and hurt he had caused. When the third day passed, Alma the Younger awoke (see Alma 36:10).

During this period, Alma the Younger had come to a place of wholeness as he experienced the Atonement of Jesus Christ and the purifying refinement of repentance. He spoke unto the people and said: "I have repented of my sins and have been redeemed of the Lord; behold I am born of the Spirit" (Mosiah 27:24).

He continued testifying of the need to repent to enter the kingdom of God and taught that by being born again in Christ, he had been redeemed from the gall of bitterness and bonds of iniquity. He had been racked with eternal torment, but his soul was pained no more.

From that time forward, Alma went throughout the

land teaching the people of the joy he experienced through Christ. He testified of God's greatness and glory. He served and proselyted with the very same sons of Mosiah with whom he had previously spread wickedness and falsehoods.

"And they were instruments in the hands of God in bringing many to the knowledge of the truth, yea, to the knowledge of their Redeemer. And how blessed are they! For they did publish peace; they did publish good tidings of good; and they did declare unto the people that the Lord reigneth" (Mosiah 27:36–37).

The Savior taught in Matthew 5:43–44 that we should "love our enemies," but this is often difficult to do. Mormon knew that the true source of love comes from the Father. He taught: "Pray unto the Father with all the energy of heart, that ye may be filled with this love, which he hath bestowed upon all who are true followers of his Son, Jesus Christ" (Moroni 7:48). In essence, as we become true followers of the Savior, we can pray for our enemies and be filled with His love. In praying for our enemies, we are blessed with the ability to love them in a way that could only be accomplished through first turning to the Savior.

President Gordon B. Hinckley taught: "Most of us have not reached [a Christlike] stage of compassion and love and forgiveness. It is not easy. It requires a self-discipline almost greater than we are capable of. But as we try, we come to know that there is a resource of healing, that there is a mighty power of healing in Christ, and that if we are to be His true servants, we must not only exercise that healing power on behalf of others, but perhaps more important, inwardly" ("The Healing Power of Christ," *Ensign*, Nov. 1988).

Both my African American and Caucasian backgrounds have had a great impact on not only my physical characteristics but also on the way I see and experience the world. In my youth, I was the only student of color at my school and only saw people who looked like me on TV. I knew I was different, but regardless of that, I felt welcomed almost everywhere I went.

When I was almost twelve years old, my family moved out of my home state of Washington, and the narrative I was used to changed. I was still very much the minority, but the state I moved to had more diversity across multiple ethnic backgrounds than the area of the Spokane Valley that I had moved from. Seeing so much diversity was exciting, and I was hopeful that I would make friends who could relate to how I had felt over the years. I think this desire is part of what made my experiences in my new town so difficult.

We lived in a close-knit community, and I made friends over the summer quickly, which came as a relief after leaving my life behind at such a pivotal age. When I started middle school, I was nervous but prepared, knowing I had friends from my ward and neighborhood attending school with me.

The year started out well. I immersed myself in my studies, friends, and the volleyball league. I could not wait to finally leave Primary behind and become a member of the Young Women program. I had very few worries and so much to look forward to.

One day on the bus, I heard a group of girls speaking angrily about someone. They expressed deep hatred for this person. The more I listened, I realized they were planning to ambush this person and attack them. They delighted in each step of their plan as it came together. Sitting a few seats away, I tried to ignore the vile language, but with every word, a sickening feeling swelled within my stomach that I could not shake.

Arrival at school was typical. I walked into the building and unloaded my belongings into my locker. Normally my friends and I would meet up before school started and walk the halls, talking about all the important things that happen in middle school, like who likes whom and what we were going to do that weekend. I stood and scanned the hallways to find them. As I rounded the corner near my history teacher's classroom, I saw the girls from the bus approaching with a crowd of ten to fifteen high school students in tow. I tried to slide out of their way, having heard their plans of attack on the bus and wanting no part of it. It was then that I realized the girl they hated and planned to attack was me.

In what seemed like an instant, I was surrounded. I looked in every direction but there was nowhere to go, no refuge. The words they screamed inches from my face should not be written. Words that have long since been penned in history books and marked for removal from daily vocabulary. Words that brought images to my mind of hatred, captivity, abuse, and murder. The words reserved only for racism and hate. These were now the words laced in between threats on my life. They were now more personal than they had ever been and stung in a way my twelve-year-old spirit had never felt before.

I searched desperately for an adult or teacher who I could call out to, but I couldn't see anything through the crowd that surrounded me. They stood so close that I could feel their breath on my skin and felt their arms pressed up against my back.

It felt like the torture went on for hours but was likely only minutes. The principal emerged from his office at the sound of the bell and the crowd dispersed with the promise to carry out their threats after school. The rest of the day was a blur. I could not focus or think clearly.

As my last class came to an end, nausea twisted in my stomach and a lump formed in my throat that made it impossible to breathe deeply or even talk louder than a whisper. I waited until the classroom was completely empty and sheepishly walked up to the teacher's desk. I explained that there were students who were threatening to beat me up after school and I needed help. He peeked out the door and didn't see anyone, so he sent me on my way.

I had waited in his classroom so long after the bell that the hallways were nearly empty. I hurried out to the bus lane and instantly, I was encircled yet again. This time, they had gathered a huge group of the student body and created a single-file circle surrounding me. I searched frantically for a friendly face as the crowd yelled racial slurs and threats, but I could see nothing. My vision blurred completely, and I could not make out a single detail. My ears started buzzing and I could hear only a few isolated words yelled from the crowd. I felt like my legs were going to completely collapse. I couldn't move. I couldn't speak. I felt like I was spinning. I had lost control of my body out of total fear. I had never felt that way before, which added to my terror.

At the time, my bus picked up the high school students before it came to pick us up at the middle school. Normally, the high schoolers talked and waited while paying no attention to us out on the grass, but this day, for some reason, boys from my ward saw what was happening and convinced the bus driver to allow them to get off the bus. They placed themselves around me like human shields and ushered me onto the bus. They put me in a seat next to the window and filled the rows in front of me, behind me, and next to me. They didn't say a word. Neither did I.

I just sat staring out the bus window. Gentle tears rolled down my cheeks as the heroes surrounding me were berated and mocked for sitting by a Black person for the entire forty-minute bus ride home.

In many ways, to me, these young men are another example of those disciples who were numbered among the three hundred and eighteen in Genesis we spoke of in an earlier chapter. They were secure in who they were, they knew what they believed, and they had made choices throughout their lives that made it possible for them to act when I needed them most. They had chosen to live in a way that allowed them to be my humble, unnamed heroes. So humble, some of them have now said they do not remember that day at all, giving the glory of the rescue to our Heavenly Father, who sent some of His sons to comfort His frightened daughter.

The boys stayed by me as I walked home and didn't leave until I was in my house and collapsed into my mom's arms, where I finally freely sobbed.

Now I knew, at twelve years old, what it felt like to have someone hate me because of the color of my skin.

This was the beginning of a challenging year. Some of the attackers were also members of my ward, and I felt like I could not escape. A couple Sundays after this event, we had a combined Young Women lesson. The leader stood at the front of the room prepared to teach and opened the lesson by saying, "Anyone who marries outside of their race will be damned, along with their children."

I was the only person of color in the ward, and I felt every head turn to stare at me. The lesson went on as the teacher shared quote after quote to substantiate her claim. She even said that by being attracted to someone of a different race, we would be committing great sin.

I sank so low in my chair, I wanted to disappear into it. I had never heard these teachings before and, as the faces of boys I thought were cute crossed my mind, I suddenly felt so overcome with shame. I had been sinful and didn't even know it. I couldn't believe that I was learning these things now! How could I have lived my entire life as a person of color and never been told this? I was hurt, angry, and lost. I thought what she was teaching had to be true as she used scriptures and quotes of prophets carefully crafted and twisted to pull me further and further into the deep depths of despair. I had always been taught I was a loved child of God, but never had I been told that I was bound to laws that others were not because of the color He had created me to be. I had thought I knew Him, and in that moment, I became very unsure.

My parents and later my bishop emphatically renounced this lesson, but I still struggled to overcome the shame that came from desperately misguided insight.

Each day dragged on after that, and though I was surrounded by kind people, somehow the feeling of being hated seemed to take over my every thought. One woman began waiting in her car by the bus stop and would drive by me as I walked home, calling me names. On one occasion, she threw something out the car window, barely missing me, and I did not go back to see what it was.

I thought for sure that the friends who were protecting me would eventually turn away. They too were beginning to experience the abuse. Those who sat by me on the bus were mocked for sitting by someone of my ethnicity and wore targets on their backs for supporting someone who was different.

I often remember these days as the time I prayed in school nearly every second. Every thought also included a cry out to God. As a result, divine intervention and deliverance followed.

I began to pray for those peers and others in my community. I prayed with vigor and committed to read my scriptures daily for the first time in my life. I tried to not speak about people in a negative light and continued to trust in a God who had already delivered me once. I realized quickly that He was the God I had always known, not the imposter they had spoken about in Young Women that Sunday.

Finally, summer approached and the school year ended. I had respite from the daily attacks. With newly called Young Women leaders, it began to seem as though church activities were more bearable, too. As girls' camp approached, I was apprehensive yet determined to attend.

The fresh air came as a blessing. Each activity that year focused on the worth of souls. I began to find a renewed sense of love for myself that came through the Atonement of Jesus Christ working on me from the inside out. But that was not the only soul that grew in worth to my heart. I began to feel the love promised in the scriptures when we pray for those who hurt us. I began to feel compassion and understanding for people who had caused so much trouble and hurt for me.

At the end of the week, we were given the opportunity to share our testimonies of the Savior. My palms were sweaty and my heart seemed as though it would pound out of my chest as I stood to share the words that were written upon my heart by the Holy Ghost. I shared my testimony of the Savior and that I knew He loved me. I talked about the previous year and the heartache it had caused. I told my fellow young women of the all-encompassing deliverance that comes only through Christ's Atonement—of my healed heart, my comforted spirit, and my ability to forgive. Tears flowed as I testified of the greatness of God. Following the meeting, those who had once encircled me in anger approached me yet again. My heart began to race until I looked into their tear-filled eyes. They wrapped their arms around me and sobbed. They pleaded for forgiveness and spoke words of appreciation for my patience and kindness. They shared that they now had a better understanding of the love Heavenly Father had for them because of the testimony I had shared.

I was hugging people who I had once believed to be my enemy, all because of regular faithful prayers to a God who loves each of His daughters. I learned for myself the sacred truth taught by President Dallin H. Oaks: "The Savior's teaching to love our enemies is based on the reality that all mortals are beloved children of God" ("Love Your Enemies," *Ensign*, Nov. 2020). I don't know the burdens my sisters were carrying that year, or if they had fears and pains of their own, but I knew then, as I do now, that they are incredibly loved by their Father in Heaven.

Racist behavior is never an acceptable answer, regardless of one's circumstance, and it was not my job then, nor is it now, to teach others about the impact of such harmful behaviors or how to overcome prejudices. That work must take place in the heart of each individual through personal searching, study, and repentance through the Atonement of Jesus Christ. However, I knew that whether those around me chose to change or not, I needed Jesus to heal and change my heart, too. I needed Him to teach me how to forgive what felt impossible, and how to see myself like He does. Sharing my testimony that night was an opportunity for me to connect with Christ and to bear witness of His infinite ability to carry me through my hardships.

The change of heart those in attendance felt was not because of me, nor should it have been. It was because they had opened their minds and hearts just enough to learn and be corrected by the Spirit. I do not know what learning they had embarked on before that day, nor do I know what the decades to follow have brought in their growth—that isn't my story. What I know is that my Savior, Jesus Christ, can take my darkest moments and use them to show how much He truly loves me.

In the end, the months of prayer and fasting were not for them as much as they were for me. They connected me with a Father in Heaven who heard my cries and a Savior who knew exactly how I felt and met me in my fear and heartache. These pleadings for people who sought to hurt and destroy me taught me the worth of souls and prepared my heart for the opportunity to embrace, forgive, and love in a way that more fully aligned with the love only granted by my Savior and His Atonement.

Years later, I married the high school boy who had sat next to me on the bus that day while I cried—a man who is not my race but loves me and loves God. The leader who gave that lesson came to our reception. She hugged me and wished me well. We have never spoken about her lesson that day. I hope her heart changed over the years, but if not, mine did. She may not know it, but she taught me to love God and to rely on Him when it seems there may be no one else to trust. Through her misunderstandings of gospel principles, doctrine, and history, I learned to place my faith in Him, not in the actions of leaders, ward members, or my peers.

Now I have four children, each with different and beautiful skin tones. One by one, they have learned about racial injustice and have come to me in fear and disgust for the things those before us have lived through. I have sat with each of them crying in my lap, horrified by our nation's past and worried over things most of the children in their classes do not think twice about.

My children have asked if they or their siblings will ever be hurt because of other people's racism and hate. I wish I could promise them that the world is different than it used to be and that biases have changed, but I cannot bring myself to say those words. I can't bear the thought of giving my children a hope that may be dashed, causing them to lose not only faith in the world but trust in their mom. Instead, I teach them, one by one, that we have a Heavenly Father we can each rely upon no matter the persecution we face or the pain that comes from the news headlines.

Feeling wronged or attacked is part of the human experience. This experience in my life has been trumped by far more damaging betrayals over the years, and I have heard the gut-wrenching tales of so many others that go far beyond anything that my twelve-year-old self experienced. However, the message is the same.

The burdens we all carry can teach us to rely more fully upon the Savior as we embark on our individual journeys. When we experience feelings of the adversary creeping into our thoughts, it is an opportunity to strengthen our relationship and resolve with God. In so doing, we will see the worth of all souls—not only our own—in an entirely new light. Unity with God unlocks the door for each of us to meet our full potential. This potential is met both through the power that comes from offering loving forgiveness and the strength and humility provided when we feel loved, repent, and are forgiven.

I think back to the priests who prayed for Alma the Younger. I wonder if Alma the Elder really needed them to pray for his son or if they were the souls who needed the connection that comes through praying for those who may have hurt them. I wonder if those prayers prepared them to love the leader Alma the Younger would become and to know their God so much better. To me, those priests are heroic disciples because they were willing to pray for men who seemed unsavable.

Each of us will experience times in our lives when we need others to pray for us. We will each have moments when we say unkind things and need to be forgiven by our fellow men. I know that I have sought and required forgiveness far more often than I have needed to offer it.

The people who forgive me when I seem to be unforgiveable to myself are amongst my team of unknown heroes. These everyday disciples teach me by example, through prayers and fasting on my behalf, of the love of Jesus Christ.

I know that you have been hurt. There are people who have combined against you or who have broken your heart. Perhaps you have fasted and prayed and sought every day, maybe even moment by moment, to feel the healing of the Savior's Atonement and to be blessed with the sacred power to forgive. As you have done so, you, like the priests of Alma, have served as a daily disciple. You have learned what it means to pray for your enemies. And little by little, you have learned more about how to love as Christ loves.

Living as a disciple of Christ is so much more beautiful as we remember to pray for all of God's children. When we take the time to see others as Heavenly Father's children whom He loves, we can begin to feel the compassion He has for them. We can start to understand why He is asking us to forgive, and we may find that our fellow men are not our enemies at all. They are like each one of us, searching for our place and striving to know the plan the Lord has for us. When we pray for our enemies, we become like the unnamed scripture heroes in the story of Alma the Younger, providing an opportunity for the Lord to testify to us the worth of every soul.

"Remember, the worth of souls is great in the sight of God" (Doctrine and Covenants 18:10).

ACT AS EARTHLY ANGELS

The incredibly obvious yet often overlooked heroes in the scriptures and throughout Church history are angels. Angels come to help faithful members overcome the enticements of the devil, warn of impending danger, testify of Christ, comfort, assist individuals through their repentance, interpret dreams and visions, and protect prophets from antagonistic brothers, fiery pits, and lions' dens. Angels came to cheer the hearts of mothers who long awaited the birth of children and even announced the coming of the Messiah to young Mary and Joseph.

Angels sang at Christ's birth and comforted Him in the garden. Angels have even played a pivotal role in the Restoration of the gospel on the earth in the latter days.

Sometimes we learn the names of these angels, but more often they heed the call given to them by the Father and quickly help and bless, leaving their names unknown and giving all praise and glory to God.

Alma the Younger received a visit from one of these

nameless angels, who accompanied him as he repented and turned his heart more fully to the Savior. He went on to serve an incredible mission and left his place at the judgment seat to serve exclusively as a high priest and preach the gospel. In Alma chapter 8, he came to the land of Ammonihah and began to preach. However, the people were entrenched in their traditions of Satan and did not receive Alma, his preaching, or the Lord. Instead they cast him out of their town.

Alma's heart was weighed down with sorrow, and he found himself heavy with tribulation. As he pondered in his sorrow, the very same nameless angel who had helped him repent appeared to him again. The angel said to Alma: "For thou hast been faithful in keeping the commandments of God from the time which thou receivedst thy first message from him. Behold, I am he that delivered it unto you" (Alma 8:15). I think it is so touching to imagine that the Lord saw a brokenhearted Alma who had more work to do and He sent someone familiar, someone who knew him, someone who understood. It is as if the Lord sent Alma his own personal angel. I think the Lord sent Alma a friend.

First, the angel encourages Alma to rejoice. I wonder if Alma struggled to see where the source of rejoicing could come from. He had left his life behind to teach the gospel, and instead of being heard and received, he was reviled and cast out. He was mocked for the very thing he loved and believed the most, the beliefs that defined who he was. He watched as people turned away the same power that had saved him. Despite all of that, the angel told Alma to rejoice because of his faithfulness in keeping the commandments of God.

Heavenly Father sent Alma an angel to first provide comfort in his willingness to live and love the gospel. Then, the angel told him to go back and preach to the people and warn them of their impending destruction if they failed to repent. Upon hearing this, Alma returned speedily to the land.

Alma didn't saunter; he returned speedily. I like to think that he was able to return with haste because he had faith that had been built upon past experiences. The Lord sent Alma the same angel friend who had helped him trust in the Savior's redemptive grace before. Maybe Alma could return with haste because he knew and was reminded that he could trust in God again.

As soon as he entered the land again, he was hungry and in great want of food. This was when he met his future mission companion, Amulek, who had been struggling with his own faith. Amulek received him, saying, "Thou art the man whom an angel said in a vision: thou shalt receive" (Alma 8:20).

A nameless angel prepared the way for Alma to receive sustenance and a companion. I don't know if it was Alma's angel or if Amulek got an angel of his very own, but to me, there was no doubt that God was aware of them and their mission and prepared a way for each of them to be successful. Amulek received Alma into his home, and Alma was filled.

The two men followed the call of the Lord, which was carried to them from the mouths of angels, to preach to the people. Some repented and became pure in heart through the Atonement. However, others became increasingly angry. The evildoers were so enraged they gathered the believers, including the women and the children and their holy scripture, and burned them alive in a painful death while Alma and Amulek were forced to watch in utter horror.

Alma watched people he had been called to serve and Amulek witnessed the people he loved die a horrendous death and suffer unimaginable torture. I have tried to place myself there and imagine what that would feel like. The sounds were probably so horrendous as the victims cried out for rescue, and the flames may have burned a deepening hole of revulsion into these men of God as they felt the heat pound on their faces. I can only imagine a darkness that was so heavy it settled on their shoulders, making it hard to even stand. I cannot begin to imagine the grief. The solemnity of loss is so significant, even the scriptures do not go into detail. This is one scripture story I just can't stand to stay in for long.

As I picture the scene, I imagine that perhaps an all-loving, all-knowing God preemptively sent angels to witness what He needed these men to do so when they looked on in anguish and disbelief, they knew there was someone greater leading the charge.

Maybe the Lord sent them angels so they could remember that their Heavenly Father was aware of them and the innocent souls that suffered. I like to believe that these same angels were the first to hold and welcome these innocent children into their heavenly homes.

I believe in a God who still sends angels. He sent angels to Joseph Smith throughout the Restoration and possibly sends angels to prophets and apostles throughout time to continually teach, warn, expound, and prophesy. For most of us, though, our angels reside on this side of the veil—brothers and sisters who comfort us through their willingness to love and serve like Christ. Unnamed, angelic disciples.

Elder Jeffrey R. Holland spoke of such people in his talk "The Ministry of Angels" when he said: "When we speak of those who are instruments in the hand of God, we are reminded that not all angels are from the other side of the veil. Some of them we walk with and talk with—here, now, every day. Some of them reside in our neighborhoods. Some of them gave birth to us, and in my case, one of them consented to marry me. Indeed, heaven never seems closer than when we see the love of God manifested in the kindness and devotion of people so good and so pure that *angelic* is the only word that comes to mind" (*Ensign*, Nov. 2008).

I have the sacred opportunity to be a mother to children

with disabilities. It is a calling I feel underqualified for, but it has awarded me the most sacred experiences for learning and gaining a better understanding of how uniquely the Father loves each of His children. Through my children, I have met many individuals who I believe are truly angelic.

I didn't always understand this role and calling. When I was a young mother, I wanted to do everything right. I had my first son, Tatem, at the ripe old age of nineteen, and I desperately wanted to prove that I was ready and able to be his mother. I felt the stares and whispers of doubt follow me throughout pregnancy and believed I had something to prove.

Tate was a healthy and beautiful baby. He looked just like me, and I was so excited to have a little son to dress up and spoil. I spent every waking minute teaching him. First to hold his head up, then roll over, crawl, and walk. He met these milestones more quickly than most babies, and his little soul had me beaming.

As he grew, we noticed that his speech was not developing. He would try to speak, but nothing was ever clear enough to even begin to guess what he was trying to say. As weeks and months wore on, he began to show signs of severe social anxiety, and simple tasks became almost torturous at times.

It was impossible to take him to a friend's house for dinner or playdates because the change in people and environment would paralyze him in fear; I would often just leave, feeling completely defeated.

Sometimes people would call him spoiled or bratty and suggest that he was just throwing tantrums. But I was his momma. I could look deeply into his gorgeous, dark brown eyes and I just knew he was so confused. I knew with every part of my soul that my son had a story that he desperately wanted to tell but had a brain that at this point was unable to tell it. My son wasn't a spoiled brat; he was a child of God calling out for help.

So, I began the search for that help. I spoke with the pediatrician, and little Tate was evaluated for speech therapy. They told me he was too far behind for speech and started with play interventions instead. The weeks turned into months and the play therapy yielded no results. He did not say a single word, and his poor anxious heart was not stilled. He needed a new approach.

I returned to the pediatrician and expressed my concerns again. It was such a relief when she listened to me and didn't question what I felt he needed. She referred us to a different speech pathologist at the children's hospital, and I scheduled an appointment the moment we left the doctor's office.

Tate and I walked into the evaluation, and I was pretty nervous but hopeful that we would finally get some answers. The kind pathologist began her evaluation but was unable to hold his attention or elicit any different response than we had seen from play therapy. She didn't seem to command the room, and it appeared as though Tate was leading the session, not the therapist.

I went home feeling like there would never be an answer. I was so frustrated. I prayed for Tate that night, just as I had many nights before. This time, though, I did not ask Him to help Tate talk and I didn't ask Him to heal. I just asked for an angel. I asked my Heavenly Father to send me the right person, realizing now more than ever that Tate truly belonged to Him. He would know who to send to care for the son He had sent me. That night I prayed with my whole heart to find the person who had the knowledge, resources, and time to teach me what Tate needed to succeed.

And He did.

The next day, I called the hospital rehab center and asked if there was another therapist who would better fit my son's personality. The woman on the other end of the line found an opening in the schedule of their lead speech pathologist and, like magic, fit us right in.

The miracles that followed were astounding. God really did send us our angel. Tate and I spent hour after hour, week after week, year after year in a tiny room with an amazing angel who taught us how to find Tate's voice.

Each new word was a celebration in our home as Tate's world and life expanded. Our child who had once seemed to be a shell of a boy blossomed, and we watched as his spirit was free to express what had been kept inside for so long. The journey was arduous, but the blessings were innumerable.

During this time, we also became the parents to little

Zane through foster care adoption. Zane was tiny and perfect, and we loved every drop of him. He was born with Down syndrome and congenital cataracts. This meant that the lenses of his eyes were so badly scarred that instead of seeing his precious brown eyes and pupils, there was only cloudy whiteness. It also meant that instead of seeing the world around him, little Zane saw only darkness.

We took him home from the hospital and care of the NICU with an appointment scheduled for the ophthalmologist at the children's hospital in the days to come. Zane was given a doctor with patients who traveled up to six hours to see him because of his knowledge and expertise.

This doctor got to know our family and did everything he could to help Zane have the best eye health possible. He went out of his way to help me feel empowered to meet Zane's needs.

During Zane's first eight months of life, I was only his foster mom, unable to complete an adoption until later. Before one of his surgeries, I sat with him bundled up in a blanket waiting for his birth mom to come see him before he was taken back. We waited and waited, but she had still not arrived. The doctor came to take Zane back, and I explained that we were hoping his birth mom could see him before surgery.

Without knowing the turmoil my heart had faced for weeks as I wondered if I would be Zane's mother from one day to the next, this kind and wise doctor looked into my eyes and said: "You are here. You are loving him. You are caring for him. You are doing everything. You are his mother. No one can say otherwise."

They were the exact words I needed to keep going and keep trying through great uncertainty.

It turned out that Zane would require multiple surgeries to correct the cataracts and improve his vision. In his first eight months of life, he endured eight surgeries, most of them eye related, and we became well acquainted with the surgery staff at one of the best hospitals in the region.

One of Zane's first few surgeries as a newborn was to improve the strength of his trachea. Individuals with Down syndrome often suffer from low muscle tone. This impacts everyone differently. For Zane, it meant that his airway was floppy and weak. When he slept, he sounded like a monster truck revving its engine before a rally; breathing for him was intensely laborious.

Unfortunately, during the surgery, his heart rate dropped and complications ensued that to this day have never been fully explained to me. All I know is that as a result, he was taken to the pediatric intensive care unit, or PICU, to be monitored and remain intubated.

We had expected this to be a simple, same-day surgery. We were not told to plan on anything else, so I had come to the hospital alone while Tanner worked from home and cared for our older kids.

I ran through the multiple doors and hallways in the

PICU until I finally got outside and found cell phone service. I called and explained everything to Tanner, hoping to come up with a game plan together. As I waited for him to speak, I heard a hushed reservation in his voice. Then he explained that he had been called by the military and was expected to report to military service the following day for an undetermined amount of time. My heart and stomach dropped as I realized I would face Zane's recovery without him.

The days that followed were filled with multiple trips to and from the hospital. My selfless mom and mother-in-law consistently picked up my slack by caring for three-year-old Tate and my two-year-old daughter, Emerson. Zane would often show encouraging signs of progress and would then slightly regress and require further attention.

I was becoming overwhelmed and completely exhausted. I had recently learned that I was expecting our fourth child, and my body was achy and in need of relief. When the day came that Zane was expected to come home, I learned that he would do so on an NG feeding tube.

NG tubes run up through the nose and down into the stomach, where the formula is directly deposited. As part of Zane's low muscle tone, it was determined that he was aspirating formula into his lungs instead of swallowing it into the stomach. If left untreated, he could face pneumonia or even drown during a simple bottle feed.

I was absolutely terrified. The nurses tried to teach me

how to place and care for the tube. They cautioned that if done incorrectly I could accidentally run the tube into his lungs and cause great harm. I did not feel like this was a task that I could handle. I sat on the stiff and unforgiving hospital rocking chair, cradled tiny Zane, only a few weeks old, and sobbed and prayed and sobbed some more.

Then came a soft knock at the door and in walked my angel. I was in the depth of despair, and the Lord heard my cries and sent me the very same angel. Someone who knew me better than some of my friends, someone who knew my mother's heart, and someone who loved my family. The perfect angel—Tate's speech pathologist.

After all the years we had spent together in therapy, I didn't know that she also worked as a feeding therapist at the hospital. All of Tate's sessions had been held at an off-campus location, but the Lord knew. He knew I would need this angel more than once.

She comforted and taught me again how to care for the feeding tube. She set up feeding therapy sessions with her in the very office Tate was still attending.

It took a little bit of practice, but I became confident in my ability to place and take care of the feeding tube, and Zane seemed to thrive on it. In fact, because the tube was attached to a continuous feed pump that ran all day and night at a very slow speed, I was able to fill the machine before bed, and he would sleep peacefully through the night. Not only did the Lord provide a way for me to learn what

I needed to, He provided a way for my pregnant body to get the rest I needed to carry the burdens placed upon me. What had once seemed like an insurmountable trial now was an answer to more of my prayers.

Tanner returned from his service a week or two after we got home from the hospital, and Zane made great progress. With the help of our angel, he eventually transitioned from the feeding tube to thickened liquids to eating like a child with typical development.

When Zane was eight months old, he was officially adopted, and two weeks later, Drake was born. We became a busy household full of four children under the age of four, and we were thankful for and enjoyed the journey we were on. Zane continued to see the ophthalmologist, ENT, and other specialists, but we were blessed with healthy, happy children.

About five years later, we were given a trying week. One Monday morning, my oldest son, Tate, woke up with his eye swollen and bulging out of the socket. It looked as though it was being pushed forward by something behind it.

My mind instantly imagined the worst when my son who had been healthy the night before woke up unable to open, move, or see out of his eye. Unsure what to do, I called Zane's ophthalmologist and explained Tate's condition. Hearing his symptoms, they set up an appointment for an hour later, the exact time it took for me to drive from our home to the children's hospital where the doctor's office was located. Before rushing out the door, seeing we had no time to call for another priesthood holder to assist in a blessing, Tanner gave Tate a father's blessing, and we were off to the hospital.

We entered the doctor's office and were ushered back to meet with one of Zane's doctor's associates. We were told that Zane's doctor wasn't available that day. We were only in the room a few minutes before the doctor determined that Tate had orbital cellulitis and would need an emergency CT scan and admittance to the hospital for intensive treatment and possible surgery.

Tate had been incredibly brave, but hearing this news unlocked the floodgates. His tiny seven-year-old body shook in nervousness and his eyes flooded over in tears.

I had always prided myself in my ability to stay strong during emergencies, saving my tears for the pillow and solitude that followed afterwards. However, seeing my sweet-hearted Tatey cry and tremble made my tears flow with his as we were escorted to the emergency room.

As soon as we were settled, I started texting all our family members. They immediately started praying for Tatem—I could feel the prayers quickly bounce back down to us in that tiny hospital room. Tate had been in immense pain, but the prayers made it more bearable, and the scan came back suggesting that inpatient treatment without surgery would be sufficient to treat the condition.

Every doctor, nurse, and technician that visited our

room that day asked in amazement how I had been able to get a same-day appointment with ophthalmology. One doctor even shared that she'd had to wait over eight months to get her own daughter an appointment, and she was friends with the head of the ophthalmology department.

I smiled and knew it was no coincidence—we had a heavenly team helping us along.

That evening, Tanner came to sleep with Tate, and I returned home completely exhausted and worried about my son who was still in great pain. I closed my eyes, but I do not think I slept one single minute.

The next day, I prepared an overnight bag and gathered some of Tate's belongings and headed toward the hospital. As I entered, a thought came that I should take the stairs up to his room. I know for a fact that this thought was not mine. I am not really the type to count steps in a day—I just feel lucky to make it through most of the time. But I turned course and headed for the stairs. As I reached the top, Zane's ophthalmologist greeted me. He is one of the people who like to set record-high step counts, so looking back, it is no wonder that this is where I found him.

He pulled me aside and said that he had spoken with his associate about Tate's condition and had taken it upon himself to review the treatments prescribed and to ensure he got the absolute best care. He gave me his personal office number and told me that if I needed anything to call him but that he would stop in to check on Tate regularly, even though he was not his attending physician.

The Lord sent me the same angel when I needed him yet again to comfort, teach, warn, and provide.

That week was long. On Tuesday night, I lay awake in the hospital bed next to Tate as an extremely painful case of strep settled into my throat. I left the hospital in a hurry the next day and stopped for much-needed antibiotics on the way home.

On Thursday, Zane had yet another eye surgery, and I now had two sons in the hospital. I spent the day bouncing between their bedsides. Thankfully, surgery went smoothly, and Zane went home that evening. On Friday, Emerson's eye began to swell too. I rushed her to the instacare doctor on my way to see Tatem in the hospital, and she was diagnosed with periorbital cellulitis, the stage of infection that comes before orbital cellulitis sets in. Because we caught it early, she was able to be treated with medicine and intervention at home. That was a huge relief! I don't think either Tanner or I could handle many more nights on a hospital couch! Finally, by Saturday, we were all back home and recovering, and things seemed to be improving.

Saturday night at dinner, our youngest son, Drake, started crying. He took a deep breath with chewed carrot in his mouth and instantly began choking. We had cleared airways countless times due to Zane's eating troubles, but this time was different. Neither Tanner nor I could secure his airway, and time was dwindling. Drake's eyes pleaded with ours to do something and his face slowly darkened into a shade of purple.

I called 911 as Tanner ran down the street with Drake in his arms and pounded on the door of our EMT neighbor's home at my request. He was frantic, and of course the neighbor was initially confused, but he rushed them into their home and began working on Drake.

Despite our neighbor's efforts, Drake's airway remained obstructed. The EMT tried every move and pounded fiercely on Drake's tiny chest, but his body grew more limp, and his once warm, pink cheeks and skin began to turn cold and gray. Tanner and our brave neighbor turned to each other and felt as though Drake's departure from this life to the next was likely. I was standing on our front porch watching down the street helplessly. I didn't want to leave the other kids alone, but I desperately wanted to be with Drake. All at once, I completely collapsed and cried out in sobbing pain—I felt as though he was no longer with us at that moment. I pleaded with our Heavenly Father to save our sweet boy.

The ambulance came and those paramedics took over and were miraculously able to get him to begin to breathe again. Somehow in the middle of it all, I had texted my parents to tell them Drake wasn't breathing, and we needed their prayers. My mom was out of state but began praying with all her heart, and my dad rushed to our house. He walked up the front steps and I collapsed into his arms without a word and completely fell apart.

I had always been a daddy's girl, and he was the exact person I needed in that moment. He helped me regain my composure enough to walk down to the neighbor's house, unsure what I would see when I arrived. I walked in to see Drake propped up and on oxygen in his dad's lap. I scooped him into my arms and felt his weak, tired body collapse against me and I held his cold, blue hands in mine. He is the most talkative child I have ever met. He can tell you anything about everything. But he would not talk to me. He just looked at me while I cuddled him, both of us still in total shock.

Drake was loaded into the ambulance, making him my third child in the hospital that week. Tanner rode with him and I planned to gather what he needed and follow behind later. I was still so exhausted from the case of strep throat and the nights spent on hospital beds all week. Tanner called me and said that they had begun to prepare him for surgery to remove the remaining pieces of food that had been aspirated into his lungs when he again began to cry. He cried so hard that he coughed little pieces of carrot out of his lungs. When they checked again, they found that his lungs and airway were completely clear.

The Lord sent me more angels through our neighbor and first responders to warn, comfort, and protect. But I also believe He sent angels from beyond the veil to preserve Drake's earthly mission.

The months that followed were filled with moments of gratitude and guilt. In fact, the same emotions return when I reflect on that week. The friends who we had gone through the temple preparation classes with and who we had witnessed be sealed in the Salt Lake Temple during our "Temple Tour of 2018" had lost their amazing teenaged daughter mere months after their sealing and soon before Drake's choking episode. She had passed suddenly from a natural medical disorder no one knew she had. She was seemingly fine that morning but returned to be with the Father before supper.

They called us as she was being rushed to the hospital. We dropped all we were doing and drove as quickly as we could to meet them there. I will never forget where I was on the highway when my phone rang the second time and I answered. Her dad screamed the words: "She's gone! She's gone!" We sobbed together for a moment and then he hung up to go tell her twin and younger sister the horrifying news. When I got to the hospital, I ran into the emergency room and we just hugged and cried. It felt completely unreal.

The doctors gave everyone one more opportunity to go in and see her. We stood with her family and the bishop in that room as sacred words were prayed and shared. I felt like she was standing right next to me; it was as though it had happened to someone else.

It was a solemn honor to be included in her funeral and to spend countless hours mourning with her family. We spent many late nights around the same table where months before we had discussed the sacred ordinances of the temple, remembering beautiful Kala and imagining her taking her place with the Father far sooner than anyone could have fathomed.

Her passing is so heavy and was still so fresh at the time of Drake's emergency. As they loaded him into the ambulance, I stood with Kala's mother on the driveway as we each wiped away tears of remembrance for the sweet girl she had already lost, and how close we had come to reliving the same nightmare.

As our hearts mourned in agony with them and our prayers always contained their names, it was hard to understand why we had been spared such a loss when they had not. I felt unworthy and broken at my inability to understand God's law and individual plan for each of us.

This takes me back to the story of Alma and Amulek. As they stood in agony at the loss of the righteous women and children in Ammonihah, Amulek turned and said: "How can we witness this awful scene? Therefore, let us stretch forth our hands, and exercise the power of God, which is in us, and save them from the flames."

Then Alma responded: "The spirit constraineth me that I must not stretch forth mine hand; for behold, the Lord receiveth them up unto himself in glory."

"Behold, perhaps they will burn us also," came Amulek's reply.

"Be it according to the will of the Lord. But, behold,

our work is not finished; therefore, they burn us not" (Alma 14:10–13).

The Lord sent angels to Alma and Amulek more than once to prepare them and carry them through the journey that He had for them. They attempted to follow the Father's will with exactness, but even still, heartbreak came.

The Lord has sent me angels more than once to prepare and carry me through the things that would follow. I do not know or understand the heartbreak that came to my friends. I do not know why their daughter's work moved from this side of the veil to God's and why Drake's work remained here for a season longer, much like Amulek did not understand why he lived while his friends and neighbors perished before him.

But I believe in a God who is there for each of His children. Kala's parents have shared that angels have come to them in Kala's passing. They also saw the hand of the Lord in their lives as He prepared them to enter the temple and learn more of His redeeming love so soon before she was called home. I like to believe and imagine that the people of Ammonihah were prepared in their own way, maybe even by their own angels, prior to their horrendous deaths as well. One thing I can say for certain is the God I know has a plan for each of His children and meets them all in their times of need, often through His angels.

Through these experiences, I have come to know that even when we are doing all we can, heartbreak will still come, and the winds of trial will still tear with severe velocity across the landscapes of our lives. But the Lord will send angelic disciples to carry us through. He will send them more than once, and He will send them in different ways to each of us, but He will send them.

Thank you for being one of those angels to our brothers and sisters in the gospel. When you send a kind text message of support, you are someone's angel. When you share a thought or testimony, you are serving as a quiet angel. When you pray for the brokenhearted or show up over and over again for those who need you, you are living like the same angel who showed up for Alma more than once.

We can serve as the Lord's everyday disciples as we heed His call to offer love and support to His children. I believe that there is nothing more sacred than being permitted the opportunity to assist our Heavenly Father in answering the prayers of His children. Striving each day to serve like the unnamed angelic disciples in the scriptures allows us to be listening, prepared, and in tune to help those who are crying out to God with their whole hearts. Our Father is ready and willing to entrust in us the sacred duty of assisting in answering prayers. Angelic disciples are willing to answer the call to serve more than once, to comfort, carry, warn, bless, and protect their brothers and sisters in the gospel. Angelic heroes show us that God does not ask us to do hard things alone.

SEEK THE LIGHT OF CHRIST

Ammon. The scripture hero in the book of Alma that the boys love to talk about and the Primary lesson that is often most remembered. He bravely entered the land of Ishmael, got captured, was offered a wife but agreed to be a servant instead, gathered the king's lost sheep and then gathered them again, killed some bad guys with a sling, and chopped off the arms of the rest. Then he went on to take care of the horses and chariots and waited to be called in to talk more with King Lamoni (see Alma 17–18).

There is no doubt Ammon was a pretty incredible missionary. He was full of insurmountable faith in the mission he had been called to serve and went forth boldly and under the explicit direction of the Spirit. It is no wonder we like to study and remember this story. It is remarkable. But it is only the beginning.

King Lamoni called Ammon in, and Ammon saw Lamoni's countenance had changed and turned to leave. Then, the servant looked to him and said, "Rabbanah, which is being interpreted, powerful great king . . . the king desireth thee to stay" (Alma 18:12–13). This indicates that King Lamoni and his servants believed Ammon to have a power great enough to be called by a higher title. Ammon and Lamoni sat in silence for an hour. Finally, Ammon spoke the thoughts and concerns of King Lamoni as taught to him by the Spirit. As he did so, King Lamoni finally asked if Ammon was the Great Spirit.

That part breaks my heart. It appears the king believed that he was standing before his God and felt unable to speak until spoken to. I think about standing in that room for that hour as a once fearless king sat pondering. I can feel a lump well in my throat as he tried for so long to consider whether he would speak. I wish I could whisper in his ear that everything was okay, or somehow calm his heart, which was likely pounding hard in his chest.

Soon after Ammon and the king conversed, the king fell to the earth as if he were dead. I wonder if it was because God wanted to teach King Lamoni one on one about His love for him. Maybe God was making time to be with His child and dispel the perceived myth that He was unapproachable. Maybe He just needed King Lamoni to know he was perfectly loved. Of course, I do not know what all that time was used for, but I love to imagine what it may have been like to be swept away in the Spirit of God.

The king's servants took him and laid him on a bed, where his family mourned over him for two long days until the servants expressed to King Lamoni's wife, who I like to call Sister Lamoni, that he was beginning to stink and needed to be placed in the sepulcher.

This is where it gets really good. Sister Lamoni was following the small promptings of the Spirit before she was even taught what it was. She had the impression that her husband was not dead, and she followed it. She called for Ammon to come teach her more. Talk about amazing faith.

Ammon came, and the queen asked him if her husband was dead. Ammon knew that King Lamoni was having the darkness removed from his eyes and that the light of God was filling his soul in its stead. He told Sister Lamoni that the king "sleepeth in God," promising that he would awaken the next day (Alma 19:8). Sister Lamoni believed and waited. As promised, King Lamoni arose the next day and spoke of the Savior, who was to come through Mary, and His redemptive power through His death and Atonement. Upon hearing this, both he and Sister Lamoni sunk down to the earth again.

What would that have been like to see? One second everyone is fine, then they're falling to the earth as if they are dead the next. Those who witnessed this began to feel fearful. They hadn't been taught the ways of God or seen anything quite like this but began to cry out unto God for understanding. Then, they too were struck down.

Except one. One who had been waiting for this moment to testify of God. Abish. She had been converted for many years on "account of a remarkable vision of her father" (Alma 19:16). We don't know if the father had a vision that he told her about or if she had a vision of her father that taught her about Christ. Either way, through her father, she had come to learn and be introduced to the gospel and was then converted unto the Lord herself.

For years Abish had worked with fellow servants and for the king and queen and was unable to share this sacred testimony that filled her heart. Upon seeing the Lord teach the people in this way, she felt compelled to run.

She ran from house to house hoping to finally share the good news of the gospel. Unfortunately, the people were less enthused and thought Ammon had caused death and carnage and was frankly up to no good.

Once again, Abish's faith and testimony took over. She walked over to Sister Lamoni and touched her hand, and the queen instantly stood (see Alma 19:29).

Incredible. The impossible made possible through Christ.

Surely Abish's wise father had been a faithful disciple, sharing his testimony with his daughter that she would know the goodness of God. So was Sister Lamoni. She stood by her husband during his time of learning, begrudging him nothing, and had the faith to learn and turn more fully toward God herself.

Sister Lamoni could have easily hardened her heart against King Lamoni. She could have said that if not for his poor choices in the past, he wouldn't be assumed dead or causing pain and disruption from his repentance process. Instead, she listened to the Spirit, received the testimony of her husband, and sought to learn for herself.

I remember the first time I walked into a room full of modern-day Sister Lamonis. My friend had invited me to attend the meeting, but I had felt apprehensive. What if they didn't want me there? What if I didn't feel welcome? What if I took away from the meeting or made others feel uncomfortable? But she insisted, and so on that Wednesday afternoon, I obliged. Though uneasy, I went with my friend to my first Addiction Recovery Support Meeting for Families and Friends of The Church of Jesus Christ of Latter-day Saints.

My friend's son had been struggling with addiction for years, and her heart was quite heavy with this trial. We had gone on countless trips to the temple to add her son's name to the prayer roll. When she learned about the support group, she wanted me to join her.

We walked in and the spirit of these sisters hit me like a wave. Sisters with smiling faces and Christlike demeanors sat in a circle and lovingly welcomed us in as we found our seats. That night, as we talked about our Savior, we laughed, we cried, and we remembered His sacrifice for us and for those who may be struggling.

I left feeling more spiritually fed from that meeting than I had felt from any other meeting in my life. Something about these sisters was different, and I wanted to learn what it was. I wanted to be like them.

Week after week and month after month, my friend and I returned to the support group. I heard stories from mothers, wives, and grandmothers who were each carrying heavily burdened hearts at the hands of loved ones who suffered from addictions of all degrees and types.

As they shared their stories of betrayal from their loved ones, I expected their responses to be those of bitterness or even hate. From what I knew at the time, it seemed as though these kind sisters would be fully justified in these feelings. In fact, these sisters were now women I considered to be among my dearest friends, and I felt protective of them. If they didn't feel angry at the hands of their addicted loved ones, I would feel the anger for them!

These sisters spoke so plainly and perfectly about the Atonement of Christ, there was no denying that they understood the principle better than most. Surprisingly, though, they talked most often about how Christ's Atonement had saved them in their own sin. They talked about daily repentance and the consistent need to turn more toward Christ every day. They shared how their loved ones' addictions pushed them further and further into the love of Christ and how their loved ones' repentance journeys only encouraged them to further pursue forgiveness for themselves. They were brave enough to stop and see the darkness filling their own souls and unashamedly seek the light of Christ to replace it.

These sisters, who I saw as nearly perfect victims, saw themselves as daughters of God who needed Christ most.

They shared their testimonies of the Atonement of Christ working in the lives of their loved ones. They talked about how their loved ones' countenances changed, how they seemed more open, more loving, and more honest in all things. They talked about how their loved ones had come to low points in their lives and often feared speaking to their God.

I heard sisters share how their hearts would break as their loved ones, possibly like King Lamoni, would feel inadequate to even speak to the God that created them and loved them perfectly. In fact, these sisters, while pained from the choices of their loved ones, spoke of a Heavenly Father who loved these individuals so completely that He allowed them to walk through an experience that helped them to know Him better. They shared that maybe they were going through this trial together because God wanted to teach their loved ones individually about His love for them. Maybe their loved ones were "struck down" in this way because it was the only way that they would be able to be carried away in the Spirit and learn more about the love of God for themselves.

Maybe God was making time to be with His children. Maybe God just needed their loved ones, entrenched in addiction, to know they were perfectly loved. These women knew that God worked and healed in mysterious ways and were willing to fully subject to the ways of God to heal the hearts of the people they loved the most.

Only after they sought their own forgiveness did these sisters bear the most perfect example and testimony of the ability to use Christ's Atonement to forgive those who had wronged them. These sisters taught that through Christ, all things could be overcome. I was sitting in a room full of sisters who had experienced some of the most unfathomable, difficult, and heart-wrenching things I have been able to imagine, and they were able to focus their thoughts and feelings expressly on Christ.

Through the Savior's Atonement, they testified of their ability to stand by their children, grandchildren, and husbands whose choices had completely broken their hearts, because they had come to see as Christ sees and love as God loves. In fact, to the world their loved ones "stinketh," but to them, they were "sleeping in God" (Alma 19:8).

These beautiful, strong women gave their hearts to the Lord and allowed Him to do the healing. They shared testimonies that signified that they knew He understood their pain.

President Dallin H. Oaks taught this sacred principle as well. He said: "Our Savior's Atonement does more than assure us of immortality by a universal resurrection and give us the opportunity to be cleansed from sin by repentance and baptism. His Atonement also provides the opportunity to call upon Him who has experienced all of our mortal infirmities to give us the strength to bear the burdens of mortality. He knows of our anguish, and He is there for us" ("Strengthened by the Atonement of Jesus Christ," *Ensign*, Nov. 2015).

These sisters had experienced great anguish, and they testified that as they did so, their Savior was there for them. Like Sister Lamoni, they had faith in God and were traversing an unforeseen experience with the faith to know that God works miracles. They did not see their loved ones as lost or dead in spirit; they knew better. They knew that through Christ, their loved ones were being brought to see the light. Even more than that, these sisters were seeing that they too had reason to fall before God and be taught by and through Him. They stood beside their loved ones and waited for God's power to work miracles, and when it did, or rather, *while* it did, they fell before Him themselves.

It has been years since I walked into that first meeting. I have returned to the same meeting in different areas with different groups of sisters. What I learned from that first group tends to hold true across every group with whom I have met. Inevitably I find a room full of women who know their God and their Savior so intimately that you feel His presence in theirs. These are a group of sisters who have traveled through unquenchable darkness and in turn were saved through the light of Christ. There is a light that shines in their eyes—a light that cannot be hidden (see Matthew 5:14).

Each sister, like Sister Lamoni, had an Abish. They all told stories of a faithful friend who stood on the sidelines watching and waiting to share what the Lord had taught her long ago. These women had ministering sisters, friends, sisters, mothers, cousins, and ward leaders who were there to touch them on the hand while they rested in Christ.

The Abishes in these sisters' lives were ready to run to share the good news of God's grace the moment they had the chance. I believe the Abishes in their lives also had loving people who had taught them the gospel and prepared them for their time to testify, just as Abish's father helped her become converted unto the Lord many years before others would need her testimony.

There will be times when we are like King Lamoni, needing to be taught before God. We may also be like Sister Lamoni, ready to learn and grow ourselves. There will be times when we share our testimony and faith like Abish's father and other times when, like Abish, we hold on to faith for years before we are called upon to act. Regardless of what role we are called upon to play, the Father asks us to see our Savior in all of it and to rely upon Him as our source of light.

Part of being a disciple of God is standing amongst others who are coming to know the Savior and His redeeming grace in differing ways. We draw closer to the Savior as one of His disciples as we, like Sister Lamoni, are willing to fall down and be taught of God while others we love do the same. Humbly coming to know the miracle of His Atonement alongside our fellow men creates room for all in the fold of God.

If you are walking alongside others while they seek healing and strength, you already know what it is like to be an everyday disciple. There may be times when your heart is so heavy for your loved ones it is almost impossible to move forward, and you want them to know what you learned long ago. As you sit beside them, learn with them, and allow Christ's Atonement to work in your life and theirs, you will serve like an unnamed hero. Daily discipleship requires us to stand by those who are seeking the light of Christ while striving to become healed through Him ourselves.

REMEMBER

Helaman chapter 5 uses the word *remember* fifteen times. So, what does it mean to remember, and why is it so significant that our thoughts are turned to remembrance?

President Spencer W. Kimball taught: "When you look in the dictionary for the most important word, do you know what it is? It could be: 'remember.' Because all of you have made covenants—you know what to do and you know how to do it—our greatest need is to remember. That is why everyone goes to sacrament meeting every Sabbath day—to take the sacrament and listen to the priests pray that they 'may always remember Him and keep His commandments which He has given them.' Nobody should ever forget to go to sacrament meeting. Remember is the word. Remember is the program" ("Circles of Exaltation" [address to Church Educational System religious educators, June 28, 1968], 5).

In Helaman 5, Nephi was serving in the judgment seat. But much like Alma, he saw the wickedness of the people and gave up his judgment seat to another worthy man so he could teach the words of God. He had observed that the people had become wicked and were nearing the point of destruction, and he chose, with his brother Lehi, to teach them. As they served, they were brought to the remembrance of the things their father Helaman had taught them.

They remembered that they were named after the Lehi and Nephi who had left Jerusalem. They remembered the words of King Benjamin, who taught that there is no other way to return to God than through the atoning blood of Christ. They remembered the words of Amulek, who taught that the Lord would come to redeem His people *from* their sins, not *in* their sins.

They also remembered the admonition of their father: "And now, my sons, remember, remember that it is upon the rock of our Redeemer, who is Christ, the Son of God that ye must build your foundation; that when the devil shall send forth his mighty winds, yea, his shafts in the whirlwind, yea, when all his hail and his mighty storm shall beat upon you, it shall have no power over you to drag you down to the gulf of misery and endless wo, because of the rock upon which ye are built, which is a sure foundation, a foundation whereon if men build, they cannot fall" (Helaman 5:12).

Using these teachings as a reminder and testimony, they went forward in faith and preached the word unto the people. They went to the lands of Gid, Mulek, and Zarahemla and taught with much power and authority from

God, and the people listened, turned their hearts to God, and began to repent and be baptized.

In fact, they taught and baptized eight thousand Lamanites! They probably could have packed up and gone home to deliver one of the most epic missionary homecoming talks ever! But there was more work to do, and they pressed forward to the land of Nephi.

The people in the land of Nephi were a lot less welcoming and enthusiastic about the words and messages Nephi and Lehi had come to share. They immediately captured them and threw them into prison—the very same prison Ammon had been thrown into when the people of Limhi mistook him for an enemy. Surely many prayers were offered and miracles performed within the walls of that prison by humble servants seeking to do the will of the Lord. I imagine that after holding so many men of God, that prison had become sacred in its own way.

Lehi and Nephi stayed within the prison walls for many days without food as the people prepared to end their lives. When hope seemed lost, Nephi and Lehi were encircled "as if by fire," and the Lamanites could not grab or harm them because they would be burned (Helaman 5:23).

Nephi and Lehi said to the people: "Fear not, for behold, it is God that has shown unto you this marvelous thing, in the which is shown unto you that ye cannot lay your hands on us to slay us" (v. 26).

As soon as they said these words, the prison walls shook

and nearly tumbled down around them. Darkness enveloped the sky while fear took over the hearts of the people.

From heaven came a still, small voice that did pierce the hearts of the people: "Repent ye, repent ye, and seek no more to destroy my servants whom I have sent unto you to declare good tidings" (v. 29). No sooner had the voice ceased than the walls of the prison shook again as though they might fall and the cloud of darkness remained thick among the people.

Again came the voice: "Repent ye, repent ye, for the kingdom of heaven is at hand and seek no more to destroy my servants" (v. 32). And the earth shook again. For the third time a voice came and spoke things unto the people that can't be written. The earth shook so violently it felt as though the very ground they stood upon would divide. The people were terrified.

But Aminadab, a Nephite who had learned the teachings long ago but had in time turned from the truth, stayed in that place. His soul remembered God and the prophets that had come before. He turned and saw Nephi and Lehi shining like angels. He called out to the multitude, who turned and saw them as if they were angels, too.

Aminadab saw the frightened people and said: "Repent and cry unto the voice, even until ye shall have faith in Christ, who was taught unto you by Alma, and Amulek, and Zeezrom; and when ye shall do this, the cloud of darkness shall be removed from overshadowing you" (v. 41).

Upon hearing this, they remembered what they had been taught and cried out in repentance. As they repented, they were encircled about in a pillar of fire. Nephi and Lehi were in the midst of them, and the darkness dispersed. The fire did not harm them, and they were filled with "joy which is unspeakable and full of glory" (v. 44).

As they stood together encircled in fire, repentant and full of joy, the voice spoke marvelous things to them. In nearly a whisper, He said: "Peace, peace be unto you, because of your faith in my Well Beloved, who was from the foundation of the world" (v. 47).

The heavens opened and angels came and ministered to the repentant people. These three hundred souls, who hours before had been entrenched in wickedness, were now enfolded in God's love. They were receiving the ministering of angels from the heavens because of a remembrance of the teachings and goodness of Christ and their willingness to repent.

All three hundred repentant Saints went on to teach others about the things they had seen and experienced, serving as missionaries to bring others to Christ through repentance. Many were convinced of their testimonies and teachings and put away their weapons of war and came unto the Savior and His gospel.

I love to imagine the scene of people who at first were so wicked they could not be taught at all, but as they experienced grace so pure, they were soon entrusted with the ability to teach the gospel. As they quietly remembered the leaders who had gone before and the testimony of Jesus Christ, they were able to experience growth that allowed them to carry forth His work again.

That is the power and bravery of remembering. As we remember those who have taught us the gospel, while remembering the Savior, we can experience the grace required to do His work. We can be like these unnamed disciples if we simply *remember*.

I try to imagine myself standing encircled in that forcefully strong heavenly light. I can almost feel every hair of my body standing on end as the purifying power of the Holy Ghost filled me from head to toe. My mind would race to remember my parents, my grandparents, and the Church leaders Aminadab had listed from long ago who had taught me about the Redeemer of the world. I think my ears would strain to hear the voice from heaven and my heart would plead to understand each word. It is no wonder that after such an experience, the people were able to go on to preach the word of God without fear—I would feel unstoppable after being filled with undeniable godly power and forgiveness.

Over the years, the Lord has provided my family many opportunities to remember Him. He has sent blessings and miracles that could only be seen as heaven-sent and has allowed hardships that humble me. In every instance, my soul is called to remembrance of family on the other side of the veil and of our Savior, whose Atonement covers all pains.

My husband Tanner is one of the kindest men I have met. He loves to make others feel loved and special; it is one of the things that drew me to him from the very beginning. It isn't uncommon to go somewhere with him and have him strike up a conversation with someone. As we walk away, I often turn and ask if he knew the person. He laughs and says that was the first time they had met. He has never had an enemy. His outgoing demeanor often leads many to believe that he is quite carefree. This, however, is so very far from the truth.

In his childhood, Tanner was fearful of many things. At first, it seemed very typical for his age and development. But as fears of natural disasters and other harms took over his ability to play like other children, it became apparent that these fears were greater than the average child's.

As he grew, he began to internalize and cope with these fears in a way that made things on the outside seem bright and cheerful while his heart and mind often felt a heavy, overwhelming darkness.

As the days and years passed, intrusive thoughts grew more and more intense. It started to become difficult for him to silence the painful rhetoric that filled his mind against his will. As a teenager, these thoughts became too much for his young spirit to carry, and he desired to end his life in hopes of finding peace and respite.

Thankfully, his wise parents followed promptings and quickly stepped in at the right moment. They sought the medical help he desperately required. Tanner was soon diagnosed with obsessive compulsive disorder (OCD) and anxiety disorder. These disorders manifest themselves in different ways in each person.

For Tanner, often thoughts or obsessions will be triggered by what seems to others to be an insignificant life event, like a television show, and his brain will refuse to let go of the intrusive thoughts and fears that follow. The fears will become so intense that anxiety attacks often accompany these thoughts. Some of the anxiety attacks are completely debilitating and can be physically and emotionally paralyzing. To cope, his mind will try to follow through with obsessions that attempt to destroy the fear, when in reality, they only increase it.

The most common example that people associate with OCD is the constant need to wash one's hands. In this instance, the mind might obsess over the fear of germs and cause the person to play into the obsession through compulsive cleaning and hand-washing.

While Tanner has not suffered from this specific obsession and its related compulsions, it is one of the easiest ways to describe and recognize the disorder. For him, his compulsions change often and are almost undetectable to others. He has been my best friend for twenty years and there are still times I do not notice a flare-up in compulsions right away, but I know he is experiencing an increase in obsessions just by watching the twinkle in his eye turn to despair.

He has worked with skilled doctors who have tried a combination of medications and approaches to help ease his symptoms as well as recommended books and known treatments for OCD. After applying their advice over time, he will often begin to feel relief.

Sadly, the relief is always fleeting. He is never completely free from anxiety or obsessive thoughts. He will go into what we consider to be a remission for a year or two, but the OCD will trigger again and his suffering resumes.

Over the years we have experienced many scary times together. I have become somewhat of an expert on various techniques to help during one of his panic attacks after numerous late nights in emergency waiting rooms.

On one occasion, he was so incapacitated that his body seized and tightened and he lost ability to function. His hands crumpled and distorted and his body stiffened, causing him to have trouble moving. He could not speak as his body reeled in pain on the bed. I, however, felt an overwhelmingly odd sense of peace. I kept telling myself that I should feel worry or panic, but instead, I felt total calm and knew what to do. Through reliance upon past experiences and quiet promptings, together we worked through the attack well enough to call his doctors and receive further advice.

At the time of that attack, we lived in a town with a lot

of family, all of whom were gone for various reasons. After notifying our parents of that afternoon's events, Tanner's dad contacted Tanner's uncle, our stake president, who came over late that evening and offered a comforting and incredibly inspired priesthood blessing. OCD and anxiety are so misunderstood by many people. We were apprehensive to call ward members for a blessing out of fear of being judged or treated differently. We were so thankful for a loving uncle and priesthood leader who took time from his family to serve ours.

In time, Tanner was able to again enter his version of remission, and life seemed to resume its normal rhythm for a while. However, the attacks reappeared, and Tanner continued to seek to learn methods to cope.

While he studied OCD, I felt impressed to study the writings of our Church leaders to better learn gospel doctrine and principles. At the time of Tanner's most recent recurrence, I was reading the book *Covenant Keepers* by Sister Wendy Watson Nelson. In this book, she taught about the duties and blessings of keeping our covenants. Her reminder to turn our minds and hearts to our ancestors stood out as if it were a message preserved for me. She begins by quoting President Joseph F. Smith and then goes on to give her own council:

"President Joseph F. Smith declared: 'When messengers are sent to minister to the inhabitants of this earth, they are not strangers, but from the ranks of our kindred

[and] friends. . . . In like manner, our fathers and mothers, brothers, sisters and friends who have passed away from this earth, having been faithful and worthy to enjoy these rights and privileges, may have a mission given to them to visit their relatives and friends upon the earth again, bringing from the divine Presence messages of love, of warning, of reproof and instruction to those whom they had learned to love in the flesh.'

"So, could you use a little more help in your life? If so, keep your covenants, with more exactness than you ever have before! And then ask for angels, (a.k.a. your ancestors and other loved ones) to help you with whatever you need. Or ask for them to be dispatched to help those you love!" (*Covenant Keepers: Unlocking the Miracles God Wants for You* [Salt Lake City: Deseret Book, 2016], 66–67).

This was the message I needed, the encouragement to *remember*. For years we had been relying upon prayers, fasting, and medical intervention to help Tanner through the trials he faces, but it had never once occurred to me to ask my Heavenly Father for help from Tanner's ancestors beyond the veil for assistance. I needed to remember them. I needed to turn my heart more fully to the heavenly angels that had the knowledge and ability to help.

One sunny afternoon I sat out on our front porch and pondered these words and council. The question came to my mind: "But who do I ask for?"

In recent weeks, I had determined to complete a

Mother's Day project of a beautifully designed family tree going back eight generations for my mom, mother-in-law, and myself. The project took hours as I read and recorded each name, birth date, and death date. In the process I began to read the stories of these ancestors and felt an increased kinship to them.

The names of our ancestors I had painstakingly noted weeks before ran through my mind as I considered the prayer and fast I was offering. Then, instantly, the Spirit spoke to my soul so perfectly. Grandma Norma.

Grandma Norma was Tanner's maternal grandmother. She lived in his home through his entire teenage years as her husband required extra care in a nearby facility until his passing. She was the sweetest woman; I feel honored to have known her for so long.

Grandma Norma was warm and kind. She served as the "Primary grandma" for the ward and would come to Primary to read stories and sing songs with the children on occasion. It was not uncommon to walk into Tanner's home and hear Grandma singing a folk song from her youth while folding a basket of laundry that may or may not have made it through the wash.

Tanner loved visiting with Grandma in her room and walking with her to church. I loved hearing her daydream about winning the Publisher's Clearing House sweepstakes and how she would share the money with all of her grandchildren.

Yes, Grandma Norma was the lady I needed to ask for. She had passed away while Tanner was serving his mission, just days apart from our beloved prophet President Gordon B. Hinckley. That had been a heartbreaking week for Tanner, and he dearly missed both wise, caring leaders.

I closed my eyes and began to pray to the Father, in remembrance of our ancestors, for Grandma Norma to be permitted to come to assist Tanner at this time. I had barely opened the prayer and not even had the time to speak her name when I could feel the answer and her presence instantly. Our angel had been notified. It was as though she had just been waiting for us to ask. I felt so strongly that she desperately wanted to help, we just had to seek assistance—we had to remember.

My prayer lasted a long time. I was afraid that if I opened my eyes or ended the prayer prematurely, I would have to say goodbye to sweet Grandma Norma all over again. I sat, I pondered, and I waited.

Before long, the duties that come to a mother of four beckoned to me and I stood, resolving to continue to rely on the people who love us the very most, the unseen heroes on the other side of the veil waiting to help.

In the days that followed, Tanner's demeanor began to shift, and a lightness I had not seen in a long time began to reemerge. He had found new treatment ideas and was implementing them in his daily life. He shared that he felt a renewed ability to face what he has been given.

I had not told him about my conversations to the Father about Grandma Norma until now, but I know she has been close by. I know because I have my husband and best friend back.

Tanner and I have learned together that this is a trial that he has to bear for a purpose we haven't yet been taught. Certainly, we have learned to enjoy the good moments and feel thankful for our Heavenly Father, who provides much-needed relief. We also know that it is likely the trial will resurface for years to come. We don't know when or how the hardships will reappear; we only know that they will.

Perhaps it is for us both to be again humbled to a remembrance. To remember our Father in Heaven, who always comes in our darkest days to offer relief through priesthood blessings, medications, learned doctors, and wise family members.

Maybe it is to remind my loving husband that while he is the hero to so many, the Father still needs him to rely on our Savior to save his soul. And maybe these experiences recur to remind us to look forward with faith to the glorious day that will come when all will be made right—when all infirmities will be corrected and when, through the Atonement of our Jesus, Tanner will be perfectly healed. What a glorious day that will be, and oh, I can't wait!

Like our brothers and sisters who stood in a pillar of fire with Nephi and Lehi, encircled about with angels to be refined, we have found in our marriage and family that we can use OCD as an opportunity to remember our own refiner's fire. To recall our minds to the miracles of repentance and implore us to look to the heavens to ask for our very own angels to come forward and minister to us, to teach us the things that cannot be written, to connect us with heaven, to remind us that this earthly mission never was intended to be traversed alone—to help us remember. He comes to us and assists us in our efforts and offers the reminder that He gave to His children long ago: "Peace, peace be unto you, because of your faith in my Well Beloved, who was from the foundation of the world" (Helaman 5:47).

Often, I think we see the task of remembering our ancestors as a difficult chore or another item on the to-do list. We might say things like, "There is a time and season for everything, and it is not my time or season for family history work." I know the computer programs can be tricky, it can seem as if our family's work is already done, and it can be really, really, hard to get started. But regardless of our time or season, we can be like the unnamed disciples who listened to Nephi and Lehi by simply remembering. We can remember our ancestors' stories, their efforts, and all they sacrificed for us. We can remember that our nose looks like theirs and that we have the same talents they had. We can be everyday disciples by allowing them to be angelic heroes in our lives. Every time you retell their stories, whisper prayers that contain their names, or hope to be a little more like they were, you are serving like a disciple of Christ who remembers.

Like the people of Nephi who gained strength from the memories of those who had gone on before them, we too can access strength that comes only through remembering. I believe our place in the fold of God can be richer when those we love are remembered, invited, and standing nearby. Everyday disciples remember one another, whether from heaven looking down or from earth looking up.

GIVE ALL THEY HAVE

After performing many miracles during His earthly mission, Jesus crossed the Sea of Galilee and entered into a desert place, in the city called Bethsaida. Once there, a multitude of people began to form and followed Him, having heard and seen His many miracles. The Savior received these people, taught of God, and healed the sick of their infirmities (see Luke 9).

I imagine the hours passing by as they sat in the pounding light and heat of the desert sun, marveling at the Savior's teachings. I think of His words taking precedence in their lives and hearts as they forgot their other desires and duties.

As time wore on, the multitude became in need of food. The Twelve suggested to Jesus that He should send the multitude away that they might go to town to acquire the food and supplies they would need for that night. The Twelve, as well as the multitude, knew that because they were in a desert place, they could not simply go fish or find their own food but would need to acquire it from the surrounding towns and country.

The Savior, seeing the multitude and desiring not to send them away, spoke to the Twelve, saying, "Give ye them to eat" (Luke 9:13). The food among them was scarce—so much so that Andrew said, "There is one lad here, which hath five barley loaves, and two small fishes" (John 6:9). The Savior then instructed that the five thousand sit upon the grass as He offered thanks to the Father, blessed, and broke the meager offering for the multitude. When they were filled, the Apostles gathered the remaining loaves, as Jesus had requested that none of the fragments be lost. Jesus took this very small offering, performed a miracle, and spiritually and physically fed and sustained thousands.

I think about the "lad" in this story. Being in a desert place, it is likely that he had put in great effort to acquire these loaves and fishes. Maybe he came upon the gathering by chance and stopped to listen and hear the message. It may even be possible that this was the first time he had heard of the man Jesus. We do not know, but what we do know is that this lad chose to give all he had to Jesus. It seems as though he had the faith to know that if he gave all he had, it would be multiplied by the Savior of the world.

I wonder if he knew that whatever plan he had for his five loaves and two small fishes, the Savior's plan was greater. Wherever he was going, whatever he was doing, whomever he may have been planning to help or bless, this lad was able to experience something far more significant. Forgetting himself and his own wants, this lad gave all he had, and in return, he witnessed an unimaginable miracle.

The multitude showed similar faith. They too likely had families to feed, agendas to meet, and to-do lists to fulfill. I wonder if as the day wore on, they began to feel the emptiness of their bellies but forgot the hunger and chose instead to feast upon the words of Christ (see 2 Nephi 32:3). The multitude must have known that the shops in their town would soon be closing, that the world would go to sleep, and their opportunity to meet their physical needs would be put off until the towns around them awoke again. They took no thought of this and remained in the presence of the Savior. They too had the faith to give of their time, expecting nothing but receiving everything. The multitude stayed, and as a result, they were fed. Most importantly, they were numbered among the Savior's fold.

Indeed, this lad and the multitude who were with him were unnamed disciples as they gave all they had to the Lord and waited in patient, sustaining faith.

This wasn't the first time the Savior had created greatness out of very little. While in Cana, His mother ran out of wine to serve the guests at a wedding. Traditionally speaking, this was a catastrophe. Seeing and understanding the need, Christ requested that the servants fill the pots used for the purifying of the Jews. These pots and the associated water were often used to wash the hands and feet of the Jews entering the temple; they were likely quite unsanitary.[1]

This means that Christ was using filthy pots filled with filthier water to meet the need placed upon His shoulders. He took this water and asked the servants to give it to the governor, or the ruler of the feast. It was the governor's job to determine if the wine would be used in the celebration. He declared that it was the best wine of the event and determined that it should indeed be served (see John 2).

Jesus Christ took the most disgraceful and discarded materials and turned them into the greatest wine the people could ask for.

My friends Jared and Lisa know what it means to give everything to God and let Him create miracles. In 2005, when their children were young, Jared got an ear infection and was given antibiotics to treat it. As the antibiotic filled his body, it began to shut down his kidneys. He soon was hospitalized and became completely unconscious for five days.

Lisa asked family members to come to the hospital to administer a priesthood blessing, believing Jared could be made whole. During the blessing, Jared was promised that if he got up and went to church every Sunday, he would be strengthened enough to fulfill his callings.

---

1. See *New Testament Seminary Teacher Manual* (Salt Lake City: The Church of Jesus Christ of Latter-day Saints, 2016), "Lesson 61: John 2."

Soon after the blessing, doctors predicted that Jared would make a full recovery in a few months, and the couple had faith to endure until he would experience full healing. However, as the weeks multiplied into months, Jared's condition only worsened. His kidneys went into total kidney failure. He was told he would never be able to work again and would need to be on dialysis while awaiting a much-needed kidney transplant.

This was not the promise Jared and Lisa had hoped for or expected, but they remembered the words of that very first priesthood blessing, and Jared fought to fulfill every calling the Lord had for him.

There were then and still are now some Sundays when Jared is so sick that he can barely stand, but he gets up and puts his church clothes on to attend his meetings. Some weeks, his feet are so swollen they will not fit into his church shoes, so he wears sandals instead. Other weeks, he is vomiting as he leaves his home, but still, he goes to fulfill his callings.

Year after year Jared would enter the chapel and take his place on the stand, conduct sacrament meetings, attend planning meetings, and visit his ward members in need. With each duty, the Lord gave him just enough to carry out the call. Upon arriving home, he would collapse into bed again, sometimes until the next Sunday meeting. Together Jared and Lisa knew one thing: if Jared could fulfill his calling, he would make it through that week. While this is not the answer for everyone, they believed in the counsel and promise that had been made specifically to them.

In fact, he found that as he put the Savior first in all the places he was called to be, he was carried. When he made family home evening, prayer, and scripture study a priority, the Lord gave him the strength to fulfill his calling as a father. As he and Lisa made their relationship a priority, he was able to fulfill his sacred role as a loving husband.

In 2014, Jared was finally able to receive a kidney transplant and it seemed as though things would be better. He was able to work and provide more for his family, and he continued to make Church service a priority. However, in 2018, his body rejected the transplant, and his heart is now functioning at only fourteen percent capacity. Jared now not only is back on dialysis and needs a new kidney; he also needs a new heart.

Still, Jared serves. His doctors don't know how he walks or moves about from day to day, but Jared and Lisa know that it is because they have given all they had to the Savior first. They do not know what the future holds for Jared or how long his life will be preserved.

Lisa faces the future knowing she does not have to carry it alone. She said: "I get through every day knowing that when I can't carry myself, my Heavenly Father is going to carry me. My Savior will not leave me alone. Even if Jared is not here, I won't be alone, I'll always have my Savior with me. Faith is not hoping something won't happen; it is believing Christ will be there through it all."

Jared and Lisa have raised three amazing children, who all seem to exemplify this same belief, knowing that if they give all they have to the Savior first, He will make up the difference. They have served missions as their dad has lain in hospital beds, unsure if they would ever see him again in this life, yet they moved forward with faith, still giving and still serving. Each of them has worked to fulfill their callings, just like their parents, giving everything they have to the Savior first.

As Jared's health continues to decline, often Church leaders and friends will suggest Jared be released from his high-demand stake or ward callings, but he knows that in his case, he needs the opportunity to give everything to God. The couple believes that Heavenly Father has put all the pieces in place so they could go through what they are going through and see His hand every day. They do not ask, "Why us?" Instead, they ask, "Why not us? We are so glad this was not given to someone else we love."

Lisa said when people question the time they spend serving when they could be home together, she often will reply: "The Lord can have him now. He can have the time that Jared feels good, and He can even call him home early if He needs to, because I get to have eternity. We will give the Lord mortality because He will give us eternity together in return."

When I first moved into Jared and Lisa's ward, I knew nothing of their circumstance. I only knew that Lisa was the first person to visit with me and make me feel welcome as she lovingly cared for my young son, who could not speak, in her nursery class. I didn't know Jared was so ill; I only knew he faithfully served on the stake high council and would often fill in for our ward as we needed him. I didn't know that their children were worried nearly every day about their dad; I only knew that on the days I felt I had nothing left to give, their son would come off the stand after blessing the sacrament and come take baby Zane so I could hold baby Drake and watch my oldest two children. I didn't know they were giving so much when there should have been nothing left to give.

I fear that some may hear the story of Jared and Lisa and believe that their sacrifices have been in vain. Jared's health has not improved in this life, and instead, he has gotten significantly worse. The worldly view would suggest that there is little to rejoice over when they give all they can and receive more illness and strife as a reward.

I think about when the Savior took the loaves and the fishes from the lad—the lad completely surrendered their use and fate to Him. Then, Christ blessed the offering, and He broke it. The Savior took all the lad had to give and tore it apart before it could fill its full potential. It could have appeared as though the contribution was destroyed. But it was the breaking that allowed Jesus to use every drop of the offering, leaving remnants to spare and not a fragment lost.

The most sacred and perfect offering ever given was bruised, broken, and torn, too. Our Redeemer gave all He had to the Father, including a perfect body and spirit, to create for each of us the miracle of His Atonement. He had to experience the breaking before He could fulfill His ultimate mission and potential.

As we sit in His fold as brothers and sisters each Sunday and pass trays of torn, broken bread from one soul to the next until each has partaken, we can remember that it is through the breaking that the Savior allows us to partake of every drop of love and grace He has to offer. Through our application of His Atonement, we can ensure that no fragment of His offerings and sacrifices are lost. We must always remember that it is the breaking of the perfect Son of God that made room for our broken offerings to be used that nothing be lost.

Jared and Lisa have boldly offered all they had to Christ every single day in their own way. They have had the faith to know He would bless it, and at times, He broke it. Their contribution may appear to have been ripped apart. It is in the breaking that the Savior has been able to spare this faithful family. It is in the moments of heaviness they have felt Him most. It is when they were at their lowest but able to give what little they had that they saw that through the breaking, Christ made something beautiful. And, through the breaking, not one drop or fragment of their efforts has been lost or forgotten by their Heavenly Father.

Jared and Lisa's example teaches that the Lord will always provide a way for each of us to offer all we have to Him, just as the lad gave all of his loaves and fishes and the multitude were required to give of their time, faith, and willingness to partake of the offering presented to them by Jesus Christ to receive the miracle He had for them.

Giving our "all" will be different for each of us as we face different life circumstances, phases, and challenges, but as we continually seek ways to place our humble offerings before our Savior, He will teach us where and how we can give freely to Him, in a way that is absolutely perfect for us.

Jared and Lisa have taught me that the Lord does not need our meager offerings, but we need an opportunity to give them. Jesus did not need the lad's loaves and fishes and He didn't need the dirty water to make wine. The Lord needs His people to believe in Him, to trust in Him, to rely upon Him, and put all their faith in Him. He then asks us to give Him all we have, regardless of how small it may seem or if others feel we have given too much. Only then through our faith will He create miracles out of our "all." He will give us the strength to do what we should not be able to do. He will bless what we give Him, and though we may at times feel pain in the breaking, He will gather all that is remaining, leaving behind nothing. If we give Him mortality, He will give us eternity.

Maybe that is what being a humble disciple truly is—learning what the Lord needs us to offer, then giving all we have to our Shepherd knowing that He will make great things out of our small efforts. Maybe the place He asks us to take in His fold is one of willfully submitting our wills and efforts to Him.

Through faith and trust in Christ, five loaves and two fishes can feed thousands, awful water can become decadent wine, and through Him, a faithful man and his loving wife can bless hundreds and feel carried in their service regardless of their challenges.

When you give your time, heart, and will to the Lord, you are showing Him you trust Him to use your sacrifice in the way He sees best. You may feel that after giving all you have, your offering feels as though it has been broken so much, you may not recognize it at all. Through reliance on Jesus Christ, you can remain faithful and watch as He makes miracles from the fragments. Your offering may remain unrecognizable, but it will become miraculous through Christ.

To be like the unnamed scripture heroes in these stories, the Lord asks only that we give all that we have with the faith to know He will come and provide a miracle greater than we have room to receive.

CARRY OTHERS TO CHRIST

During the Savior's ministry, He entered the land called Capernaum and the people were excited. Word spread of His presence in the town quickly, and before long, the house where He preached was filled with people. All in attendance had their own desire to learn, heal, and be edified at the feet of the Only Begotten Son.

News of the Savior's presence spread to a man taken with palsy and his four friends. We all know the part of the story when these four friends carried the man on his bed to the Savior, and without room to enter through the doors, they removed the tiles from the roof and lowered him, bed and all, to the place where Jesus stood (see Mark 2).

Think about what that would mean to the four friends. Perhaps they had heard of the Savior's miracles and knew of Him from other friends and prophets and desired that their brother be healed. I think of them charting their route, preparing the bed, and leaving families at home while they tended to their friend. Maybe these four men woke early in the morning to gather all the necessary equipment in preparation for their quest. They might have prayed for guidance before they left to carry their friend upon their backs.

I imagine they walked for miles across dusty roads, tired and burdened, but chose to press on to find the Savior. Perhaps their faith was weak, but their love for a friend was strong. I wonder if they worried that they would not arrive in time, missing out on seeing Jesus. Sometimes I like to imagine that carrying this man to worship had become part of a weekly Sabbath ritual, and now that Christ had come, they were prepared for the most important journey of all. It is exciting to think that this could have been an ordinary task leading to an extraordinary miracle.

We do not know what their journey, preparation, or personal testimonies were. We do not know their names. We don't know what it was like to carry a man onto a roof of a house, remove the tiles, and carefully lower him down, just hoping he would be received and welcomed. We do know that it was likely difficult and presented challenges.

I think about what it would be like to be one of these men. I think I would be so tired and my mouth would be dry with thirst by the time we got to the house. I think I would be so worried about completing the task that I would focus on the work more than the result. I would probably try to find the fastest way to remove the ceiling tiles so that my friend could meet Jesus and be healed. I think I would be so worried about my friend that I would not even realize that I had come to Christ myself until I saw Him through the hole I had created in the roof.

Regardless of the path they took to get there or the strength of their faith at the beginning of their journey, they ultimately found themselves at the feet of the Master. By bringing a brother unto the Savior, they themselves came to Him.

Ultimately, their faith and daily discipleship allowed them to be instruments in the hands of God, presenting an opportunity for the Savior to demonstrate the most important and significant miracle known to mankind.

"When Jesus saw their faith, he said unto the sick of the palsy, Son, thy sins be forgiven thee" (Mark 2:5).

In that moment, the man's spirit was made whole.

I like to imagine that that was the miracle the man had sought all along. When I think about the Jesus I know, I think of a Savior who asks us to choose Him and who does not impose upon us His redemptive grace. I think of the invitations He so commonly offers: "Come unto me" (Matthew 11:28), "Enter into my rest" (Alma 12:34), "Take my yoke upon you" (Matthew 11:29), "Seek, and ye shall find; knock, and it shall be opened" (Matthew 7:7). Every call is an invitation to be saved and made whole in Christ. He never comes and forces us to repent; He does not impose His Atonement on those who do not want it. He waits for us to ask.

Christ had already healed blind men and lepers, all

of whom came to Christ and asked to be healed of their physical limitations, and He gave them what they sought to receive. There are no words recorded of the man with palsy, but I believe the Savior knows our hearts. Ours is a just God. He grants unto men according to their desires (see Alma 29:4).

I think of a man on his bed, who was likely unable to say much due to his disability, who looked into His Savior's eyes with a plea and a request, a request only the two of them knew, and a request only the Son of God could grant—saving, redeeming forgiveness. I wonder if the man knew that in time, his body would age and his physical healing would give way to the frailties of life, so he sought a gift that could not be undone or erased. I cannot wait to get to heaven and ask this faithful brother to share with me the contents of his heart that day. I think only then will I know the full story of the man with palsy.

Until that day comes, I genuinely believe the man came with a hope for healing in his heart and the Savior looked into this man's eyes, called him "son," and granted him his miracle (Matthew 9:2). By so doing, the Savior made a promise to each of us that He would, indeed, fulfill His earthly mission and atone for our sins.

During the April 2015 general conference of the Church, Elder Jorge G. Zeballos of the Seventy taught: "We know the Atonement of Jesus Christ is essential to receiving forgiveness of our sins, but during the episode of the healing of the man with palsy, that grand event had not yet taken place; the Savior's suffering in Gethsemane and on the cross had not yet happened. However, Jesus not only blessed the man with palsy with the ability to stand up and walk, but He also granted him forgiveness for his sins, thereby giving an unequivocal sign that He would not fail, that He would fulfill the commitment He had made with His Father, and that in Gethsemane and on the cross, He would do what He had promised to do" ("If You Will Be Responsible," *Ensign*, May 2015).

The Savior's loving forgiveness of one soul illustrated the Savior's promise for each of us to be carried to Him and be forgiven. Perhaps the unnamed man with the palsy is an unnamed hero himself—faithfully allowing the Savior to teach of His promise to redeem.

Even the scribes in the home questioned the Savior's ability to perform so great a miracle, to which He lovingly replied: "For whether it is easier to say, thy sins be forgiven thee; or to say, Arise, and walk? But that ye may know that the Son of man hath power on earth to forgive sins" (Matthew 9:6).

Then, as a testimony to His power and ability, the Savior told the man to arise, take up his bed, and walk. The man arose, and for the first time, he walked.

Like the four men who carried their friend to Christ, we too can find Jesus in our every day. Every time we lift others, whether we physically carry their bed or sit with them in sacrament meeting, we bring them closer to an all-knowing and loving Savior. And, like these men carrying the burdens of another, with every step along the dusty path, we too get closer to coming to know the Savior and ultimately witnessing the divine power of His all-encompassing and infinite Atonement.

Years ago, when our children were young, my husband and I felt impressed to become foster parents. Months into our journey, we were blessed to care for two young girls, ages six and four.

Emily and Ella came into the foster care system when they were found alone in their motel room after many days. Thankfully, the children were physically safe. However, years of neglect had left them in severe emotional turmoil. The children had lived in motel after motel as their mother turned to prostitution to earn a hit or another day of lodging. When her efforts no longer produced what she desired, they would pack up and search for the next motel room, back seat, or sidewalk to call home.

These darling babies had never entered the walls of a true home until they entered ours. Their eyes filled with wonder as they went from room to room, unbelieving that one structure could hold so many doors and hallways and that they had access to all of it. Their little eyes saw our humble home as if it were a palace. They pulled the bedcovers up to their necks in disbelief that this was theirs to keep and that they had a place to call home every single day. They spread an infectious joy of the little things in life. Movie nights on the couch became like a night on the town, and bedtime stories were adventures into faraway lands free from heartbreak and disappointment.

Soon, the joys of the small things wore off as the heaviness of their lives set in. I do not think one can imagine the pain of a child who has been torn from her mother. We can try to write about it or share stories about it. These are all far different from feeling it. Emily and Ella felt it in every way. They felt it when they saw their mother in shackles across a courtroom and were forbidden to hug her. They felt it when the judge said, "You love drugs more than your children." They felt it as they cried themselves to sleep at night only to be awoken by their own screams and sweat beading their brows at the memory of a life they had so recently left behind. Never had I experienced what it meant to feel that kind of confusion and upset. To feel it so deeply that you become it.

They became it in their outbursts and running from the pain. Emily became it as she threw objects over the loft railing with such velocity that I had to gather the remaining children and wait outside to ensure their safety, just praying she would not harm herself. Ella became her hurt as she pulled chunks of hair from her head habitually until her bouncy, curly blonde hair was reduced to thin patches on her scalp.

We tried to heal them through hours of therapy. We

tried to distract them through trips to the zoo and water-parks. We tried to love them through cuddles and hugs. We tried to mourn with them through tears on the couch and late nights talking. Each effort would last for a moment until a memory of reality entered their minds and the pain washed over them again like a wave, pulling them into the depths of the darkest sea.

One day, the news came that they would be placed into the care of their grandfather. I was completely shocked. We had been told that they had no one and we would be able to adopt them. I had planned to make these girls a part of my forever family, and with one phone call, all those plans were completely erased.

More than ever before, I really wanted these children to know their worth and to realize their potential. I poured my heart out in hours of prayer, hoping and pleading that these children could go on to remember one thing: they are not alone.

We attend church every Sunday, and when Emily and Ella joined the family, they also joined us in our pew. They learned the songs the children in our congregation had known from birth about being children of God and songs that taught them that they were only a prayer away from safety and peace. On our last Sunday at church together, we sat in the pew as we had for many weeks before. We began to sing one of my favorite hymns, "I Stand All Amazed." As we began to sing the chorus, I repeated the words, "Oh, it is wonderful that he should care for me enough to die for me," as I had numerous times before.

In that moment I saw little Ella's shoulders begin to shudder up and down as tears streamed down her face. Wrapping her up in my arms I whispered, "Ella, what's wrong?"

"Jesus isn't dead, are he?"

"No, no, sweetheart. He died for us, but He lives again."

"I knew it, I just knew it. I knew it because I can feel Him. I can feel Him here, by me."

My soul flooded over. Since that day, I have yet to find a way to describe the overwhelming reassurance I instantly felt. It became so clear, and so obvious. These were not my children; they were not their mother's children; they were most definitely not the state's children. They were and would always be God's children. He had been guiding them, He had been holding them, His love would carry them, and He would not forsake them.

My role had been so short in their lives. I had thought I had introduced them to God, when they had already known Him. I was praying for our Heavenly Father to begin to attend these beautiful girls, when He had always been there and had no plan to leave. We simply had given them the opportunity to give a name to the God they already knew.

Every neighbor, Primary teacher, music leader, organist, child, and parent who loved, befriended, and spoke of the Savior provided an opportunity to help this young child know and better understand Him. Their quiet service created an opportunity for Christ to heal and comfort the heart of a child and her grieving foster mom.

When the day finally came to move the children to their new home, I left a note with the name and phone number for their local bishop with the promise that he would be able to direct them to the activity days program in their area. Emily had become involved in our ward's activity days and desired to continue after she moved. I hugged the kids and waved a somber, forever goodbye to children I had considered mine. That afternoon, I left a piece of my heart on the front porch of a double-wide trailer.

Months later, the phone rang. On the other end was Emily. She excitedly told me what she was going to be for Halloween and that she had gotten the monthly issues of the *Friend* magazine I had sent. Then she said her grandpa needed to speak with me and passed the phone.

Her grandpa's kind voice filled with emotion as he explained the previous months. He shared that he had always desired to attend church but without a car, he was unable to. Emily had begun attending their ward's activity days and out of nowhere, the leader had offered to take him and the children to church every week. Grandpa expressed the joy he had felt from this lifelong prayer suddenly being answered.

This activity days leader had been an instrument in the hands of God in answering prayers. I do not know her name. I don't know her story. But like the four men who carried the man with palsy, she found a way to serve. I wonder if she saw a young girl who needed to come to Christ and acted, not knowing what the outcome might be. She may have had to wake up early on Sunday mornings and prepare the route and the vehicle by which she would bring this family to church, and to Christ. This selfless leader may have had wounds in her own heart, but maybe she forgot them and pressed on. I hope that by seeing their desires fulfilled, she too was filled.

What we do know is that this faithful sister is an unnamed hero to children of an all-knowing, omnipotent God. Through her, prayers have been answered and a way provided. She will likely never know about a foster mom who six years later still prays for children she loves but may never see again. She may never know the impact her simple offering has had on a generation. Yet, her contribution has created an opportunity for Christ to show His love and goodness in abounding ways.

Her willingness to act as a disciple of Christ opened the door for the Savior to perform miracles and allowed a whole family to experience the sweet promise of the Savior's all-encompassing Atonement; a reminder that the promise made to mankind by the Savior of the world to atone for each of us was indeed gloriously and miraculously fulfilled.

We can serve like the everyday disciples in the scriptures as we seek to carry Christ's lost sheep to Him, allowing Him to comfort and save. Maybe this is, in part, why we are called to minister to one another—because we each need the simple reassurance of knowing there will always be someone waiting to carry us when we cannot carry ourselves. When you help others come to Christ, whether it is by offering a ride, sharing the scriptures, or living your testimony, you are showing you know how precious the role of a daily disciple truly is.

Quiet service shines light on God's willingness and divine ability to answer prayers as we strive to carry one another into His fold.

FEAR NOT

From these few examples, it is obvious that small things can help us exemplify the Savior. Steadfast, daily disciples carry others to Christ, have faith in the journey, pray for their enemies, have the faith to repent, lift one another's burdens, listen to others' stories, and so much more. To be a disciple of Christ, He only asks us to serve the missions He has called us to serve and to fulfill the duties He needs us to personally fulfill. That is enough. It is more than enough. It is heroic.

Nearly every story in the scriptures has people who stood bravely in the background. I encourage you to look for them, think about them, and apply their examples to your life. You will see that they were important and needed, they followed prophets, they stood strong in adversity, and they were willing to be humble and repent when it was required of them. They were needed in their story; they have a place.

You are needed in the story that is being recorded on

high today. The Lord needs brave men and women who stand beside our prophet and apostles and who are bold enough to know that they are needed in the kingdom. You may feel like you're unknown in the world, or even in your stakes and wards. You may even feel as though your story is forgotten. But I promise you, it is remembered by your Heavenly Father. Your name is written in His records and on His heart. Your contribution is sacred because your daily discipleship is the very thing that brings you to Him.

When I was preparing to go on trek as a youth, we were asked to memorize a hymn that we could think about during those long, hot days on the dusty Wyoming plains. I picked my favorite hymn and listened to it, played it on the piano, and sang it to myself constantly—in the shower, driving down the street, walking to class. Everywhere. I didn't want to miss or forget a single stanza. To me, it was and is the perfect hymn. It teaches of Christ, our missions, and our journey back to Him. This song covers it all.

It is the same song Joseph Smith requested to hear moments before the fatal shot that took his life. Joseph Smith restored the gospel, saw God the Father and His Son, built temples, met angels, restored the priesthood, translated the Book of Mormon, helped write the Doctrine and Covenants, retranslated much of the Bible, moved halfway across the country, buried children, and was the first prophet of this dispensation. Surely, he knew he was a loved servant of the Lord. Yet still, this was the song he wanted to hear and these were the thoughts he wanted to think right before he returned home to his Maker. If this was the song that was good enough for the prophet Joseph, it was more than enough for me.

"A Poor Wayfaring Man of Grief" is one the longest and most wonderful songs in the hymnbook. It starts simply with a man or woman sharing his or her testimony of service. I like to think the speaker is a fellow sister. She starts out talking about "a poor wayfaring man of grief" whom she has met in many ways and in many places throughout her life, but there was always something about him that she could not place that won her love and encouraged her to act.

She talks about giving the man her last piece of bread and though once physically hungry, her body and soul hungered no more. She met him again trying to gather water from the stream without the use of a vessel. She offered him her cup and he drank. When he returned the full cup to her, she drank too and felt that she would never again thirst.

She went on to rescue the man from the storm and, offering him her bed, slept on the ground and felt as though she were in the beautiful Garden of Eden as she rested. Later, she found him beaten and left for dead but took pity on his soul and offered healing and shelter until his wounds were gone. She had many wounds herself, but through her service she forgot her own pains.

Finally, she met a man in prison who, for lying, would be put to death the next day. He asked her if she would die in his stead. Fearful but faithful, she replied that she indeed would take on this man's punishment and the next day, her life would end.

The last verse cannot be paraphrased because of its beautiful cadence. It says:

Then in a moment to my view
The stranger started from disguise.
The tokens in his hands I knew;
The Savior stood before mine eyes.
He spake, and my poor name he named,
"Of me thou hast not been ashamed.
These deeds shall thy memorial be;
Fear not, thou didst them unto me."

—"A Poor Wayfaring Man of Grief,"
Hymns (1985), no. 29

With every small act of service, she felt relief in her own sorrows and comfort in her own pain. She didn't know why the people she had met throughout her life felt so familiar or why her soul yearned to serve so selflessly. She just pressed forward in her ordinary, seeking to love in humble faith. When her life was complete, she stood before the risen Lord, and then she knew. She knew where her place was and to whom she had always belonged. Her life, filled with daily discipleship, amounted to a lifetime of serving her Jesus and her God.

With heroism comes bravery. Bravery to press forward, bravery to serve those who may not want to be served, bravery to believe Christ will forgive and heal, bravery to remember, and bravery to follow His plan for your mission, and the Lord asks us to fear not. With every step of heroism and the bravery that follows, we are serving the Lord, and in Him, we cannot and shall not fear.

I did not get to cuddle and rock the precious newborn Christ child. I didn't meet the Savior in Cana or sit at His feet in Capernaum. I didn't kneel at His cross or see the stone rolled back from His tomb. I wasn't there when He came to the Lamanites in the Americas, and I have yet to feel the nail prints in His hands and feet. Those were not the missions I was called to serve.

But someday, I know that I will see Him again. My spirit will know Him before my eyes will. I will know the tokens in His hands and feet; I will feel the wound in His side. His glorious voice will speak my humble and unworthy name. It will be just Him and me. My tears will wash His feet.

President Nelson so lovingly taught: "In a coming day, you will present yourself before the Savior. You will be overwhelmed to the point of tears to be in His holy presence. You will struggle to find words to thank Him for paying for your sins, for forgiving you of any unkindness toward others, for healing you from the injuries and injustices of this life.

"You will thank Him for strengthening you to do the impossible, for turning your weaknesses into strengths, and for making it possible for you to live with Him and your family forever. His identity, His Atonement, and His attributes will become personal and real to you.

"But you don't have to wait until then. Choose to be one of His true disciples now. Be one who truly loves Him, who truly wants to serve and lead as He did" ("Prophets, Leadership, and Divine Law," Worldwide Devotional for Young Adults, Brigham Young University, Jan. 8, 2017).

As we seek to continue in the faith, seizing the moments we are called to serve, allowing Christ to be the ultimate hero and leader of our earthly missions, we will take our place as one of His true disciples.

When you see His kind face once again and press your hands to His, Christ will remember your good and faith-filled moments, the unnamed hero moments, the everyday disciple moments. He will remember the times you carried others to Him. He will remember when you pressed on through challenging journeys. He will remember when you prayed for your enemies, had the faith to repent, sought to forgive, listened to the stories of others, received the gospel, and every instance when you drew closer to Him.

He will remind all of us that we always had a home in His fold and were always numbered in His multitude; we simply needed to have the faith to stand firm in that place. But like our dear prophet taught, we do not have to wait until then—we can receive His loving reassurance for all we are doing to be His true disciples, now.

As we seek Him, He will remind us, and we will know for certain, that because of His perfect Atonement, our imperfect efforts will be just enough to look into His eyes and hear Him say: "Well done, good and faithful servant" (Matthew 25:23). "These deeds shall thy memorial be; fear not, thou didst them unto me."